MW00614397

COMPOSE YOUR SOUL

How to Turn Your Daily Chaos
into Calm Control

ANGELA NUTTLE

DEDICATION

This one's for you, Mom. This book was born during our mother-daughter weekend retreat in Destin. You've taught me well, and I'm thankful for our refreshing relationship. Love you…

CHAPTERS

PREFACE

I'm a quirky writer. I'm throwing that out there because you will read this book and recognize that I don't present ideas like the most eloquently skilled authors. Sounding pretty isn't my goal. I don't have a journalist's education, but I have learned to write in a way that allows readers to have fun, learn, and get inspired about making serious decisions about their lives. This is my goal for you.

I didn't create a massive, organized plan of how I would structure the book, what the order of topics would be, or even a simple outline. Instead, it came to me in random chunks of inspiration. I didn't do all kinds of wordsmithing because I wanted to preserve the authenticity in each idea. I want you to be comfortable in this book, just as I made myself comfortable writing it for you.

I'm a person just like you. I work, I have a family, I have certain talents, and I have imperfections. I have a full schedule; I feel the pressure of deadlines and have stressful moments. I juggle family responsibilities, have unusual family members, and all of those other chaotic life situations. I have also experienced wild successes and miracles. All roads I have traveled have led me to gain an in-depth understanding of what calm control is, and how to achieve it.

You will find that I have incorporated some of my personal stories so you can have examples of what I am talking about. I've learned that we are all whole people who can't compartmentalize our lives. We learn from *all* life events, which includes business, work life, family, tragedies, and spiritual experiences—it all counts.

Composing your soul isn't a simple 3-step process that can be built overnight. It takes deep reflection, brutal honesty, and the willingness to accept that you have unique DNA. All of us desire to belong in some fashion, but we don't always believe or act like others. This internal conflict is natural and important to recognize. What composes your soul might not compose mine, and what works for me will not be a perfect fit for you. It starts with figuring out what your natural state of being and fuel sources are. It's also about determining when you have the most energy, what are the *modes* that you tend to operate in, and where you tend to get stuck.

Many self-help books fall short of helping people create lasting change. I know because I have purchased a lot of books and gotten bored with 90% of them. They all have a prescriptive process to follow that rarely aligns with a person's natural state of being or algorithm—a concept we will explore later in this book. My approach is that in order to compose your soul, you have to create composure based on your values, natural state of being, beliefs, and a good understanding of your pre-existing conditions—also a concept we will learn more about later.

I am going to give you a plethora of tools, processes, and a lot of food for thought. Some things will resonate with you more than others, but you will definitely get value as you read and apply the concepts.

Be prepared to take down your defenses and be yourself. If you truly want to compose your soul and invite calmness into your life, it takes courage and honesty to dig deep inside your history and its influence on who you are today.

There's nothing wrong with you. You simply need to find the most effective and beneficial way to show up as yourself. You have everything you need, so let's get started.

CHAPTER 1

INTRODUCTION STORY: HOYT AVENUE

"Everything we do today is kindled by something that happened to us in the past." -Angie Nuttle

"You're not the boss of me."

It's a position I've held since I can remember. My mind is flooded with vivid memories of my first quest for independence, freedom, and a composed soul. It started at the mature age of 3.

I decided one day that I was going to school. I gathered my golden books, *The Three Little Pigs, Goldilocks and the Three Bears,* and *Little Red Riding Hood,* and headed down my street, Hoyt Avenue. My teenage Aunt Rosalie, who lived on the same Indianapolis street with my grandma, poked her head out of the door. My recollection is this:

"Where are you going?"
"I'm going to school."
"Oh. Okay." She shrugs and goes back inside. I think she has a boyfriend in there.

That was easy! I trot along to English Avenue toward Christian Park. My mind goes back to a few weeks earlier.

I was with my dad and uncle, standing out in the rain with a big black umbrella as they played basketball. We had been to this park several times before. The park was known for its big wading pool, and my mom took me there a few times. We stopped going because a bully kid stole my towel and my mom's way of handling the big conflict was never to come back. I was okay with that decision because on the same day, there was a giant worm in the wading pool, and I refused to get back into the water. Two traumas in one day were enough for me to stop being fixated on the pool.

It wasn't until basketball day, however, that I discovered the school. Let's face it, watching two grown men fight to put a ball into a hoop in the rain is not exciting for a preschooler. Naturally, my attention wandered, and the school was an easy focal point.

The prestigious brick building seemed huge and mysterious. There was an instant connection between me and that building, and I was determined to explore it with full curiosity somehow. I wasn't aware of any age or capability limitations at that time, so I didn't know what I didn't know. I dreamed that I was in it wandering the halls. I imagined that there was other kids there playing, making art, and getting delicious snacks. The more I created the vision, the stronger my drive became to get into that building.

So, here I am, a 3-year-old kid, looking at this magical place from across the busy street. It's real. Without thinking about it, I skip across English Avenue to the other side.

Now, any parent would be horrified knowing their preschool aged child just crossed a busy street alone, and later it seemed like my parents weren't angry or upset. At that moment, I didn't care about anyone's feelings or what the rules were.

This is my moment, and I am going for it.

I run to the big school building. Nobody is there. In fact, nobody is anywhere around the basketball courts, the wading pool, or picnic areas. It is strange, but exciting for me. I walk around the whole establishment, looking in the windows and seeing posters on the walls, books, tables, and chalkboards. My blood starts pumping with anticipation that I might be able to get in there.

I try all the doors. They are locked, so I settle in at the front door steps. I start reading my golden books, looking at the beautiful trees, hearing the chirping birds, and just *being me*. In this moment at Christian Park, no one is dictating my life or telling me what to do. I am experiencing true freedom for the first time ever, and that feeling will become a part of my life fabric.

After some time, something in me speaks, "You have to go back now." I am not sure where that voice is coming from, but anxiety creeps in. I have reached my goal, but I realize I can't freeze time. After all, hunger is calling my tummy, and I didn't bring any food. I don't fully realize how to articulate everything, but I know that my soul has been composed as I experience freedom in this place.

It was a peaceful experience that will never be removed from my memories. That moment when all was well, everything was perfect, and my heart was grinning from rib to rib—precious and timeless. My curiousness had me wondering what it would be like to get inside and walk the halls, but I would save that for another day.

It's funny how I remember the little things about that afternoon. I felt a sense of joy as I took in the bright, beautiful day. The sun's rays bleeding through the trees like shots of sparkled beams as the wind blew through the leaves. I reluctantly headed back to Hoyt Avenue, but I was living in satisfaction that I fed my emotional appetite. I crossed busy English Avenue again and started the journey back to Hoyt Avenue.

In a matter of minutes, I sense someone following me in a car. I turn to look, and it's a black and white police car.

Panic!

I speed up my pace, trying desperately to get to the next corner so I can turn off. Before I can make it, the officer gets out of his car and approaches me. He's big, almost like a giant. He asks me where I am going, and I let him know I am going home.

"What's your address?"

I don't know how to tell him; I just know where to go.

"I will get you home. Get into the car with me, and I will take you there."

I reluctantly get in, and as he starts the car, he drives past my street. I begin to implode quietly, thinking I will never see my family again. Instead, he takes me to the police station. It's a big building with lots of desks and chairs. He directs me to sit on a swivel chair.

Okay, this is a little bit fun, swirling in this chair. The police officer brings me pretzels and a drink from the machine. Other officers come over and smile at me, calling me "cutie" and "honey." I could probably be okay with all this attention.

I don't remember much after that, but I know the fun was over when Dad picked me up. I don't recall him lecturing me, or being angry. In fact, I don't remember anyone being mad or upset, but I do remember feeling satisfied that I got to go to school in spite of the consequences of getting my first police car ride.

Your Natural Algorithm

We are all looking for that place within ourselves to be composed, peaceful, and free. We want to accomplish something. We want to get there and stay there, yet the world calls us back to reality. We grow up, and our momentum dissipates when we start thinking of survival and the demands that others place on us. "How will I eat?" "Where will I live?" "What if he/she becomes upset with me?"

We go to work, punch the clock, do our time, and come home. We get caught up in what has to be accomplished tomorrow at the office, and the deadlines we have to meet. We create a deep cycle of stress as we try to navigate through this political world and the businesses that feed it. We lose sight of those energizing memories, our values, and the goals we have for ourselves.

We look back at those idyllic and distant memories so we can relive them, hoping to squeeze some life back into ourselves. There's nothing wrong with that, and you can draw strength from those memories. You just have to avoid being fixated on them if you intend to live a life of meaning and develop a sense of composure.

For composure to happen, it takes the creation and allowance of experiences (notice that it's plural, more than one), which can be extremely difficult. What's more challenging to accept is that you will have to purposely create uncomfortable experiences in order to develop resilience. I affectionately call this "jumping off the cliff."

What is the real goal? Is it to become more productive without creating more work? Is it to be at a peaceful place in your mind wherever you go? Or is the goal to fluidly move between productivity and peace? It could be these things and more. Whatever "it" is, I want to help you get there.

Most people want to live in meaningful ways while honoring their authenticity and core values. It's important to approach this personal shift in a way that *you* believe supports your mission and how you want to live your life. In order to approach and lead a meaningful life, you will benefit greatly from understanding something I call your *Natural Algorithm*.

What does that mean?

The dictionary defines *algorithm* as *a procedure or formula for solving problems based on conducting specified actions*. Another source notes that it *involves a set process or set of rules to be followed in calculations or other problem-solving operations*.

I chalk it up to this: Your *natural algorithm* is the content in your life's playbook. You will find this unique-to-you algorithm gives you clarity about your mission and living your mission will bring composure in your soul.

There are three underlying forces behind your *Natural Algorithm*: *Pre-existing Conditions*, *Written Codes*, and an *Inner Executive Committee*. These three things ultimately drive your mission, your mindset, and your mouth. We will examine all of these concepts throughout the book.

It's truly about how you like to operate in life based on who you are authentically. It encompasses all of your personal rules, boundaries, and policies you hold yourself to. Your *natural algorithm* influences your daily operation as you go about solving problems and achieving goals. It dictates your responses, when and how you rest, and why you should (or shouldn't) rest. There's also a part of you that is pre-wired to process the world in a certain way.

I have many questions for you. We will spend time in the book exploring three important questions:

- What is your *natural algorithm*?
- What does it mean to compose your soul as you embrace this *natural algorithm*?
- What can you *do* to activate your mission based on #1 and #2?

Ready to compose your soul? Let's start exploring.

CHAPTER 2

YOU'VE GOT PRE-EXISTING CONDITIONS

"All roads lead you to where you stand. Of course, nobody told you that you would wear holes in your soles, or your soul. Thank goodness for the gift of calluses." -Angie Nuttle

Take a moment to think about these questions:

- Why do you believe the way you do?
- What values do you hold as sacred?
- What are your "always" and "never" rules of engagement?

The answers to these questions are important. They give you clues about the filters you apply to what's unfolding in your life. They influence what composes you, and what unravels you. They reveal why you are content, or why you are not. They impact the way you show up, and why you may be missing opportunities to be fulfilled.

Pre-existing conditions are developed by circumstances that have occurred over your lifetime. They are milestones or experiences that have deeply impacted you, made a certain, lasting impression upon you, and affect the way you see the world in every aspect. They are the reason you enjoy certain aspects of life, and they also shape defense mechanisms that kick in when you are in tough situations.

You have at least one pre-existing condition around each of these categories (and I am listing them as they come to me, so they are not in alphabetical order because that doesn't fit my algorithm):

Family
Children
Marriage
Relationships
Money
Food
Sex
Spirituality
Conflict
Happiness
Work
Self-Expression
Physical Activity
Leadership
Crisis

These are just a few areas we all formulate pre-existing conditions around. You may have stronger feelings around one category over another. Let's use *money* as an example. Take a moment to process these questions:

Current State
- What is your current situation with money?

- What challenges around money do you deal with regularly?
- What recent decisions have you made around money?

Actions

- How do you handle money?
- What are your do's and don'ts? Why?
- What rules or boundaries do you operate by where money is concerned?

Beliefs

- What do you believe about money?
- What triggers a negative reaction to it? Why?
- What triggers a positive reaction to it? Why?

Experiences

- What are some of your earliest memories about it?
- What are some of your personal milestones where money is concerned?
- What incidents have highly influenced your beliefs about money?

Personally, I have pre-existing conditions around money and miracles. When I'm facing a difficult situation that seems impossible to overcome, I think about boats.

STORY: The Crazy Miracle Boat

25 years ago, I was a young working mother of two. I was also married to my first husband, who was addicted to drugs and was constantly wiping out the bank account. It was frustrating for obvious reasons, and I felt trapped. I was

determined to get through college because I knew I would have to make a bold move in another direction, and I wanted to be prepared to give my children a safe and happy life. In the meantime, I needed to hold things together and create some kind of normalcy for the children.

The house we lived in was my first mortgaged home, and I wasn't about to abandon it (at least not at that point). I had to strategically hide money and my only credit card so we could remain in the home, while also paying the rest of the bills.

One morning, I went to my hiding spot to get the bill money that I had stashed in a secret compartment in the wall. I reached in, and nothing was there. I reached again, feeling a sense of panic rise inside my stomach. It was gone.

To make matters worse, I found out my credit card had been maxed out. I called my husband, who initially denied taking the money, but when I confronted him about the cash withdrawal, he made up a story about how he needed it for a job he was doing and "somebody" would pay him back. The same story happened every time:

"I lent it to _____ (insert fictitious coworker) and they will pay me back next week."

Or excuse #2, the promise of a new job.

"I will pay it back when I get my next job." The money never came.

So here I sat. $1,100 worth of bills was due in the next few days. I had done everything I could do to earn back what had been spent on drugs. I sold my jewelry, had yard sales, picked up an extra temporary weekend job, and it barely put a dent in what I needed. I was exhausted and out of options.

I start praying.

"God, I've done everything I can do to keep us afloat. I can't do it anymore. I'm asking for you to provide for us. I need a miracle."

I'm sobbing, and I hear a quiet voice.

"Go to the mailbox."

I question myself.

"Did I just hear that? Am I losing it? Go to the mailbox?"

It's quiet. I have nothing to lose, so I go to the mailbox.

The day is bright and sparkly. Kind of strange, but it's like the day is smiling at me. It's comforting. I open the mailbox, and there's a single envelope there. It's addressed to my husband, and it's from *Movie Gallery*, a company that he had done some construction work for a couple of years earlier. I am curious. My heart leaps with a little hope while my mind is saying, "Oh my Lord, what is this?"

I open the envelope and find a check for $1,300. I gasp!

"Oh my Lord! Is this for real?"

I read the enclosed letter. It explains that *Movie Gallery* somehow overlooked a payment they owed from 2 years ago, and they are paying it out now. I know this is almost impossible because of how strapped the finances have been our entire marriage. Yet, I don't care about that right now.

Next hurdle: How do I get him to sign the check over to me so I can put it in the bank?

I call him to come home to sign the check so I can pay the bills. He is supposedly out looking for work, but I catch him at his friend's house, and I tell him what has happened. He comes home immediately and says he'll take the check to the bank and deposit it.

I'm nervous, but he says he'll take it straight to the bank. I don't argue with him because he has a big druggie temper that I know will turn ugly and scary.

I wait. Surely he won't mess with the check from God.

I'm thinking about how I will call and transfer the money immediately to take care of the mortgage, light bill, and phone bill. I imagine how wonderful it will be to have another month taken care of, and I can't even allow myself to think about next month.

It's been 30 minutes so the money should be in there now. I call the bank. I know the bank lady on a first name basis. Her name is Linda.

"Sorry, Angie. I haven't seen him yet."

An hour later, I call Linda back again. I can hear her pity for me. Same result. I hang up the phone. I feel sick.

"God, I know you sent that check as an answer to my prayer."

I am speaking to God in my mind, just unable to believe that He would send me that check so that it could be spent on drugs.

Three hours later, I get a call. It's him.

"Where are you?"

"I'm at Lake Eufaula. I bought a boat. Don't worry. Steve is going to pay me back next week, and I will give that money to you to pay the bills. I just couldn't pass up this deal. I will be home later tonight!"

Click. The line disconnects.

I am stunned. A boat? I can't fathom it. Yet, there is still this crazy belief in me that God intended that money as an answer to my cry for help.

"God? I know that money is for bills, I just know it!"

An hour passes. I'm cooking ramen noodles for the kids. At 10 cents a package, it's a frequent meal of ours. The phone rings. It's him again.

"Well, I'm headed back home with your money. I guess it really was meant for you."

I'm surprised, but not really.

"What do you mean?"

He is wavering.

"The boat I bought just sunk and is sitting at the bottom of Lake Eufaula. They are fishing it out of the lake now, and I am headed back to the owner to get a refund."

My heart leaps! It's true! I'm not crazy, I'm not hearing things, and God has heard me!

"Lord, please don't let anything get in the way of him making it back with that money!"

He makes it back, and the money is safely in my hands. I will never forget what has happened, and the impact it has had on my belief in God's provision of a miracle in my life.

A positive pre-existing condition has been born that will forever filter how I view money, God, and life.

"With God, *nothing* is impossible!"

—

When I think about the story I shared with you just now, I would be remiss if I didn't admit that I developed an additional pre-existing condition where money is concerned. As a result of my first marriage, I have a negative filter of suspicion and mistrust when it comes to money. I am remarried now, but I become the spending police when I think money is coming out of the account in ways that I don't approve. It's an area where I've made a lot of progress, and I continue to manage it well.

You have pre-existing conditions, too.

Think about the big milestones or experiences that are etched in your psyche. Some of your pre-existing conditions are incredibly positive; some are negative and painful. You've taken away valuable information and lessons from these experiences and created values around them. You've established beliefs because of them, and now you make decisions that are influenced by them. You may not even remember some of your experiences, but they still may be influencing how you show up now.

How to Start Working on Pre-Existing Conditions

"Change the world. No, wait. Change me, and the world will change." - Angie Nuttle

This thought bounced right into my head as I entered the gym after a very frustrating day. It was God talking to me again about my state of *Crazy Head Syndrome.*

A pre-existing condition had been showing up for me all day—one that you may be familiar with—Murphy's Law. It's an adage that states that if anything can go wrong, it will. I picked it up from my father, who was at odds with the universe and believed that it was out to get him. I will share it with you now so you can understand how to catch your pre-existing conditions in action. Here's my recollection:

Sitting in my home office on a bright Monday, I'm ready to jump into work with all cylinders firing. An hour passes. The internet goes down. Access to everything I need to work on is suddenly unavailable.

I'm huffy. I turn my chair around and my dogs, Buddy and Jovie, are having a loud wrestling match that includes intense growling. Time to walk out and take a breather. Buddy and Jovie follow me as Mom's dog, Millie, joins them to make it a three dog fan club. I understand what it's like to be stalked.

I get outside after fumbling over the dogs, and my mind randomly flashes to a picture of *Three Dog Night*, a 60's rock and roll group from my childhood. I start humming that song that could technically be my theme song, *One is the Loneliest Number*. What is going on with my brain right now? Squirrel.

I eat an apple then come back inside. I check in with my mother, who is recovering from back surgery, and I get her some coffee. I prepare my daughter Mackenzie's breakfast. Then I go back to the office, determined to get something done.

The internet is back up, but it is slow. I feel anxiety rising in my shoulders with every crawling moment. My head might explode. I have the need for work speed, and technology is grossly interfering with my natural algorithm. I'm not achieving anything. This sucks.

I feel like things are piling up. I hate that feeling, so I try to push it even harder, toggling between windows on the computer until I have about seven of them up.

I get an "unexpected error" message, and my windows abruptly close. I lose everything I just did.

Crap! If blood could boil, mine would be pure lava right now. I keep hearing this thought in my head:

You better hurry up. You're getting behind. You won't get it all done. People are relying on you. You won't be seen as credible. Do what you said you would do, or people will write you off, you'll be forgotten and invisible.

BAM! I pick up something interesting in those last two statements. I make a mental note to process these accusations from my inner critics later because the internet is back up now and I have to make the best use of my time.

I'm back to cranking it out, and lightning fast. This incompetent computer can't keep up with me. My mind works ten times faster than it does, and soon the little Apple processing disc appears to let me know I've clogged it up. This Mac hates me. It's rebelling against me.

I want to throw this computer out the window!

Mackenzie comes in and needs a ride to cheerleading. She's coordinated an extra, private lesson with her coach, and informs me we need to leave 30 minutes early.

"Hold on!" I bark at her tersely and instantly regret it.

Murphy is jacking up my life right now through this stupid computer.

"Go ahead and put the dogs up so we can go." I am hoping to buy a little extra time for one last upload. Ten seconds later, Buddy bites Mackenzie's finger, and she's crying.

My emotions explode, and I snatch Buddy up.

"What do you think you are doing? Don't you EVER bite my kid again! Get in your crate now!"

Jovie and Millie are looking at me from underfoot, and they won't move. I imagine they are staring at my eyeballs bulging out of my head, bloodshot and angry.

"MOVE!" I yell at the dogs because I almost trip over them trying to get out of my office. This is a calamity. Everything that could go wrong is happening. Murphy is here.

I put Buddy in his crate and grumble as we head out the door. What is wrong with me? The universe is out to get me today. Murphy is winning.

I am upset with myself. Why am I reacting this way? What is triggering this pile of jacked up mess that I've created today? Why do I need to go fast?

All kinds of inquiries are entering my head as I drop Mackenzie off at cheerleading and head to the gym. I'm determined to revisit those inner critics that taunted me. I also want to figure out how Murphy's Law got invited into my day.

I get on the treadmill and start speed-walking. A few minutes in, I start processing how my day has gotten terribly off track. I recognize that my pre-existing condition around Murphy's Law slipped in at the first internet outage this morning. He entered my thoughts, with a subtle warning. I revisit what he was saying to me.

"Uh oh. The internet is down. I hope this doesn't happen all day. Probably will."

Later, he was more pronounced with the second internet outage and the other irritants.

"Well, you knew this would happen. It runs in the family. This doesn't happen to normal people. Only you, Angie. Only you."

By the end of the day, he showed his face completely.

"Yep, it's Murphy's Law here. The universe is against you because you are trying to do good. I successfully interfered with your dad's life, and now I'm here to do the same to you. You are stuck with me."

I come back to my treadmill, and I bump it up a few notches. I want to erase Murphy out of my life. I imagine that Murphy's Law is a big greasy spot on the table, and I spray it with Easy Off. I wipe it away and throw away the paper towel.

Now my focus is on the inner critic that showed up. I decide that I will just *notice* as I replay the words that compelled me to freak out.

You better hurry up. You're getting behind. You won't get it all done. People are relying on you. You won't be seen as credible. Do what you said you would do, or people will write you off, you'll be forgotten and invisible.

I notice that the first few words are familiar. Maybe not exactly in their current form, but similar to something I have heard. Where is this coming from? I wait for it to manifest itself.

"Move it! Move it! Move it!"

Those words are echoing in my head from the past. It's my dad. He's always working. He's impatient, and he's always in a hurry. He is a disciplinarian, and I have to be responsible and fast at all times if I want to have some fun time with him. If I mess up, he is highly disappointed and lets me know it. I want to make him happy, so I move faster. I do more. I strive for perfection. I want to get to the fun, so I go as fast as I can. I just want to see him laughing, and I want him to make me laugh.

By the time I finish what I need to, he's too tired and our fun time is short-lived. I am rarely fast enough for him. If I could just be faster . . .

I notice a funny feeling in my chest and behind my eyes. I notice tears threatening to form in my eyes. I tell them *NO!* I can see I need to dig deeper around this because it is clearly a pre-existing condition that has found its way into my life.

I consciously tell myself that I am only here to notice. Not to do anything or solve any problem right now. I need to sit with this over the next several days.

I refocus on my workout, vowing to keep my word and explore this newly recognized pre-existing condition so I can understand how to manage it.

What You Can Do to Notice Your Pre-Existing Conditions

You will benefit from gaining a deeper self-awareness around your pre-existing conditions, and understanding how they impact your life. I'm giving you an example of how to explore them in 3 phases:

- Phase 1: Gain Self-Awareness
- Phase 2: Explore the Values and Beliefs Correlation
- Phase 3: Soak in it

PHASE 1 - Gain Self-Awareness

Reflect on the example I gave you regarding money. Do a deeper dive by answering the questions in four categories: Current Situation, Actions, Beliefs, and Experiences. For example, let's pretend that you are frustrated about your finances. Here's a high-level synopsis of how you might work through this:

1. Current Situation: You are in high credit card debt, and your spouse continues maxing out the credit cards. You keep having talks with your spouse, with no change. You are angry and vow to stop this somehow, even if it means leaving. You've closed down two accounts to prevent any more charges from happening.

2. Actions: You have always been frugal, and in general, you are a good budgeter. You have a rule that you pay cash as much as possible to avoid debt because you are uncomfortable with the pressure of loans. Plus, you don't like paying interest.

3. Beliefs: You believe that money is a necessary evil. You believe in immediately paying what you owe so that nobody can hold any power over you or take advantage of you through exorbitant fees. Losing control over your money is a trigger for you, and you feel out of control. You feel happy and have a sense of freedom when you don't owe anyone anything.

4. Experiences: When you were growing up, your parents were very tight on the budget. You learned to refrain from asking for anything special because you would get lectured on how selfish you were when you asked for that new Barbie townhouse. When Mom took you shopping, you went to the Goodwill or to the bargain outlet where you got off-brand jeans. When you got out

on your own, you counted every penny you made from your job, and you made sure your bills were paid before you bought groceries. You have a good job now, but you find yourself shopping at yard sales and always looking for debt-free solutions.

Once you walk through your money category, pick another one that is important to you in your life right now. Walk through the questions by changing the category. It's helpful to journal this as you go. Take it in like a sip of wine instead of a gallon of Gatorade. In other words, don't be in a hurry. Capture key words and thoughts that come to your mind. If you are naturally predisposed to thinking about something over time, come back to your journal pages throughout the week, refining your thoughts.

PHASE 2 - Values and Beliefs Correlation

I want to note that there isn't a "best order" of the first two phases. You can do Phase 2 first if you want, but I find it's easier to do the steps below after you've had a few "warm-up rounds" from Phase 1.

1. Create a timeline for yourself about your life up to this point. You can get a roll of paper and create a big wall map, or journal about them. There is power in creating a visual map, and your brain processes that more clearly than just putting down words. Identify key milestones in your life, key events or experiences that stick with you. Be sure to leave space on your timeline so you can add more information as it comes to mind. It's likely you will discover some memories that you've not thought of in a long time.

2. Reflect on your values. Reflect on the values that were formed with each milestone and experience. What

became important to you? What did you repel or resist? How are these values showing up for you today in your daily life?

3. Analyze your beliefs. Think in terms of beliefs you've formed as a result of each experience. What are they? Which beliefs are serving you well, and which ones aren't?

4. Process your behaviors. What are the actions and behaviors you've developed because of your values and beliefs? Are there areas where you are defensive or protective? What about places where you are more open and energized? Which of these are serving you well, and which ones aren't?

5. Examine the results. What situations are showing up big in your life right now? What keeps happening over and over? What isn't happening? What results are you happy about? Hopeful for? Fearful of? Discouraged about?

(Regarding your values, we will do more work on clarifying those in another chapter, so hold those loosely and be prepared to refine them later on.)

PHASE 3 - Soak In It

Once you process the work you've done, let it soak. Walk away and process it emotionally. It takes time, work, and self-discipline to change the experience for yourself so you can realize new results. Soak in your timeline, write in a journal, and capture the thoughts that have been given life in your head. Let everything soak into your heart. Stop and visit your heart for a while, capturing your thoughts, memories, and feelings on paper.

- When you look into your heart, what's there? What is making your heart joyful? What is making it content? What is your heart laughing about?
- Examine the flipside. What is making your heart hurt? What's painful? When tears come, what is their source?
- There is so much value and depth in stopping here to process what is going on inside you and around you. Be present with yourself.
- Notice what happens to the rest of your body as you process. Where are you sensing a reaction in your body? What does it feel like? How do you describe it?
- Notice what is happening in the air around you. What do you see around you? What in your environment is speaking to you?
- Now, focus on your environment that is unseen: the spiritual, the invisible, the intangible things happening around you.
- Notice how you react when you shift to focusing on the unseen things in your environment. What nuances are you experiencing?
- What do you know is there, but you don't physically see? Is there something spiritual happening or present?

Soaking is a very powerful exercise that can be done often. Its benefits are genuinely real and long-lasting. Whether you realize it or not, you are designed to allow this kind of rest to exist in your life. The truth is that you are reading this book because you want to compose your soul, and a good soak is nurturing to your whole being.

At first, it may feel clunky and awkward. You will see over time that it will start to become natural and comforting. Composure develops by slipping under the covers of the busy world. Underneath is a deeper place where a sanctuary is waiting to be built by you and for you. There is much work to be done in that sanctuary. That's probably music to your ears as an overly productive person, so allow yourself the time to be there and explore the possibilities.

There are other areas to explore as you go through your personal remodel, but this should keep you busy for a while.

CHAPTER 3

UNDERSTAND YOUR
WRITTEN CODE

*"It is what it is. Until someone else looks at it,
then it becomes something else." -Angie Nuttle*

Why do some people think one way, and you think another
way? How can a person look at a situation, and you see
something vastly different? What causes someone to act in a
certain way, while you act for a completely different reason?

Your written code can be equated to a brain processing
template you follow to interpret information. Where pre-
existing conditions are driven by experiences, emotions, and
beliefs, written code is driven by the way your brain is wired.
This *default* code interfaces with your pre-existing conditions.

Is It the Brain's Fault That I Can't Change?

We can partially blame the brain for making it difficult
to change, at least in the short-term. Those little neural
pathways are etched in there. It takes about 30 days to create a
new habit, 90 days to start a pattern, and 6-12 months to
establish a new neural pathway.

27

You can change, you will just want to be prepared for a workout.

You are essentially remodeling your brain when you start this process. That's why I recommend only working on 1-2 of your pre-existing conditions because more than that will likely lead to failure. Your brain will struggle from the multitasking. Willpower is great, but when it is dividing its attention among all the changes, it loses strength. People are pretty good at starting a change, but sustaining it is another story.

I strongly recommend the help of a coach, who can hold different perspectives for you, and help you come to real change. Why? Because we easily get stuck in our perspectives. Sometimes it's pride that wraps itself around you, and sometimes it's simply not knowing any other way to think about a situation. I am an executive coach who also has a coach. It's just smart.

So, there are tons of opinions and theories out there about brain wiring and why we do what we do. Personally, I believe our wiring is a result of both genetic and environmental influences. I don't want to argue about nature vs. nurture, and its impact on the way we process information. However, I do want to focus on the fact that all of us have different preferences. Those preferences tell you *what* to process, and you act upon the template that is provided. I will share what this looks like in a story.

STORY: House-Hating

My husband and I drive around and "house-hate." Don't let the term alarm you.

We started doing this early in our marriage when we were in the dreaming phase of buying a new home. We would walk around upscale neighborhoods critiquing all the houses that we would probably never own. Our budget was conservative, so we naturally had to come up with ways to curb our enthusiasm on a big custom house.

One Sunday, we had planned to go walking in a new neighborhood. I was getting ready, and Aaron, said, "Ready to go house-hating?" The term has stuck to this day. Let's check in on my recollection:

We are now building our new dream home, and we are excited. We are at the job site every day, checking out the progress. Aaron wants to drive around the neighborhood.

"Let's go house-hating." He says with a mischievous yet incredible grin.

"Okay." My mind wakes up at the thought of exploring and discovering. I'm eager to go.

We begin the drive.

As we enter the neighborhood, the various colors, styles, and shapes are dancing with my brain. I'm taking it all in, and, in an instant, I'm visually stimulated.

Aaron quickly focuses in on one house. I call it the "Awesome House."

"Ugh! That is horrible!" He exclaims with high emotion as if he had just stepped in dog poop.

"Are you talking about that house directly in front of us?" I look at the same house. It's stunningly beautiful and creative. I love the colors, the design, and the shape. He must be looking at something else.

"Yes! I can't stand those colors; too loud. The trim is jacked up, and it doesn't line up." He is grimacing in brain pain as he takes in the house.

"That house rocks! It's picturesque. I don't even see what you are talking about. The trim?"

I am flabbergasted that Aaron can't see the beauty of this house. I know he prefers less vibrant colors, but I simply don't see the tiny misalignment of the trim edges until he pinpoints it. Even then, it takes me a few minutes to see what he's talking about. I sigh.

We move on.

The next set of houses are all pretty in their own way, but Aaron doesn't like them.

"The brick is boring and is too bland on these houses. You can't see any detail." He's obviously staying true to our term, *house-hating*, as he criticizes everything. It hits me that this is his brain wiring, which is different than mine.

Aaron looks for defects, detail, and things that need to be corrected. Loud colors distract him from accomplishing this visual mission. He likes to take in one thing at a time. He approaches the houses, and life, from a critical perspective of "Here's what I don't like." It's like a protective and defensive reaction.

I take in the big picture first, synthesizing all the colors and big shapes to ensure they are aesthetically pure, and then eventually get to detail (if ever). My visual process is to bypass detail to get to the bottom line, then work my way back to capture *the why*. I approach from a positive perspective of "Here's what I like." It's like a curious and open reaction.

We both have unique views, but we complement each other perfectly. Our brains have different written codes. When faced with a choice to take in information, process it, and come to a decision about it, we each tend to follow our own code because it is natural to us. The exception to the rule is when pre-existing conditions and everyday emotions are in play. They can interfere, and they become intertwined with the processing brain.

For example, if the owner of the Awesome House says, "Aaron, here are the keys, you are now the owner of this house," Aaron's emotions are going to kick in for a moment. His response is not going to be:

"I'm sorry I can't accept this house. The trim is jacked up."
No, his mind is going to big picture mode:
"It's free? Yes, this is a great house! Thanks!"

Of course, we will move into the Awesome House and Aaron will revert to his written code after he's overcome his emotional reaction. The first thing he will do is complain about that trim and then talk me into some different paint colors. If I give in, then Aaron will move on to analyze details for corrections, and improvements.

Let's say that we are presented with this same scenario. I have a pre-existing condition around safety and the fear of snakes (I won't bother to share that traumatic experience). If we are told we can move into the Awesome House, but there are a couple of snakes in there that have to be caught, Angie Nuttle will not move into the Awesome House because it will become the Awful House. Even if they've been removed, that house will suddenly become ugly and undesirable to me. I will have to go through extensive coaching or therapy to overcome that situation. And if I do, I will still be looking for snake evidence. That house will be the Awful House thanks to my written code being hijacked by a pre-existing condition.

Your Brain On Written Code

There are all kinds of assessments out there that attempt to measure our preferences. I am certified in many of them and have researched their reliability, but the one that measures brain preferences most effectively is the Myers-Briggs Type

Indicator (MBTI)—that's if the person follows the proper instructions and is honest with answers. The StrengthsFinder assessment by Gallup is also an effective tool to identify your natural talent themes, which are tied to your brain wiring.

Quick history on MBTI: Carl Jung was a famous psychiatrist who fathered the research on our default brain wiring. Dr. Jung was a bit "off," and although completely brilliant in an intellectual sort of way, he was stuck in his head and couldn't bring the research to a practical solution for use in mainstream society. The research was later taken on by Isabel Briggs-Myers and her mother, Katharine Cook-Briggs, who methodically built, tested, and delivered the measuring tool that we know to be the Myers-Briggs Type Indicator.

Their research concluded that there are four brain-related dichotomies. When I say "dichotomies," I mean that there are two opposing sides or different forces, and you are either one or the other. A dichotomy can be like *hot or cold*. You like something, or you don't like it, or you are *male or female*. According to MBTI, we each have unique ways of:

- Gaining energy and charging up (Introversion vs. Extroversion)
- Taking in information and processing it (Sensing vs. Intuition)
- Coming to decisions on what we've experienced (Thinking or. Feeling)
- Expressing our decisions in our everyday environment (Judging vs. Perceiving)

These functions are incorporated into our written code and manifest themselves in our personal preferences. For example:

- I enjoy being with people and get energized by conversation (Extroversion). My husband prefers time away from people so he can think about what happened during the day (Introversion).
- I love playing in the world of possibility and imagination (Intuition). My husband prefers historical data and concrete facts (Sensing).
- I step back from a situation and look at it objectively to be fair across the board (Thinking). My mother thinks about the immediate impact to people and relationships, and that's how she makes her decisions (Feeling).
- I like to be spontaneous and flexible with the freedom to change if needed (Perceiving). My husband likes structure and lots of detail. He likes to know what to plan for ahead of time (Judging).

Suppose you are an introvert, you are like a phone battery that will eventually run out of juice and has to charge up through a wall outlet. You can learn to be in the presence of other people and even enjoy yourself, but you aren't going to change the fact that you need to go charge up. Once you are charged, you are good to go for another round.

Why is this important to understand? Because there are some things that we are naturally predisposed to doing, and it may look different than the people around us. We get frustrated when others don't think or even act like us. This happens in the workplace all the time. There's a dominant way of thinking that gets imposed on the employee population, and it causes discomfort. Employees become disgruntled, disengaged, and even hostile because they feel misunderstood and unheard.

Composing your soul isn't about changing someone else, it's about changing the way you respond and how you perceive people and circumstances. It's also about respecting the other person's pre-wired brain while recognizing that you can stretch your brain to process differently. You are waking up parts of your brain for more robust thinking.

STORY: The Iron-On Emoji Project

Funny story that happened while I was writing on this very topic.

My daughter was experimenting with an iron-on transfer one Sunday afternoon. Her goal was to transfer some emoji faces onto a tote bag, and so far my attempts to help her were failing miserably. She obtained a piece of transfer paper from my mom, and we tried to feed it into the printer. Every time, the printer jammed because I was feeding the paper on the wrong side. I eventually gave up and told Kenzie to get her dad to help. He flipped the paper over and got the emoji's printed. Here's the recollection:

Everyone happens to gather at the kitchen table. It sounds like this:

"I'm going to iron these on now, and I hope it works."

"Oh, don't iron on my table, put something under it." My mom spouts.

"Mom, this is a thick canvas, it isn't going to bleed."

I sigh, seeing her look of disapproval as Kenzie and Aaron look on. I get up and get the mini ironing board, which is the perfect size for Domestic Barbie, if one exists.

"I'm ironing safely now. Okay, I think it's time to peel the paper back."

It doesn't transfer.

"It didn't work! What's up?" I'm annoyed. I've ironed it to death.

"Did anyone even read the directions?" Aaron says smugly.

I laugh and explain to Mom that this is the difference between a judger and a perceiver. Perceivers are spontaneous and don't even think about using directions. Judgers are notorious for reading all instructions and creating a plan before they do anything. A minute later, Aaron gleefully exclaims:

"DO NOT USE AN IRONING BOARD!!! That is exactly what the directions say!"

We begin laughing hysterically. The instructions show not one exclamation point, but three. The whole situation demonstrates how we operate within our written code. In this case, I am pre-wired to jump in and just do it. Aaron, on the other hand, is pre-wired to plan and explore details first, then act. His neural pathways have been etched into a template that he follows daily. This is a huge part of our written code. It isn't the complete code, but it is a big influencer.

Why and How Written Codes Can Become Problematic

I get feedback all the time that if I don't slow down, I'm going to burn out.

For a long time, that bothered me. Not because I thought it was true, but because I liked working at a maddening pace as if I was racing against the clock, but people thought I should slow down—although my employers loved my work and my pace, mainly because it benefited them.

It seems ironic, but I felt the burning judgment of disapproval because I worked too fast. This is just hysterical to me.

Something has always driven me to be ultra-responsive and quick. I consider myself an expert at responding to a crisis, and I like that feeling of responsiveness. It comforts people, it helps them to feel like someone's "got this," or someone is in this with them and it's going to be okay. If I distill it down, I don't like it when other people worry. Worrying wastes time. My way of being calm is to help other people be calm.

On the flip side of this thought is the expectation and judgment that we impose on other people. We expect people to behave a certain way, we want them to think like us, and we want total harmony in our decisions and actions. We want people to be like us, and that rarely happens. It certainly doesn't work to compose your soul.

We like what we are comfortable with, and what we know. When our brains are wired a certain way, and we have pre-existing conditions, it formulates into our natural algorithm. It becomes the way we operate. Our life's playbook, remember? Anyway, it's great until we get involved with other people.

Written codes can become problematic when you interact with people who haven't learned to compose their souls. It's also troublesome when you are dealing with people who lack a high level of emotional intelligence. Marriages break up, friends become enemies, and people resort to violence because they refuse to see each other's perspectives.

In my experience with Corporate America, companies underperform because of the time it takes to work through power struggles around written codes. I venture to say that 50% or more of the time in business is spent fighting others' positions and ideas. The person in charge is typically unwilling to accept written coding that doesn't align. If it is different, it will be resisted and fought.

One reason I've experienced a fair amount of career success is because I've learned to meet people where they are at, accept them at face value, and draw them into a trusting relationship. I may not always agree with their decisions or beliefs, but I accept them as human beings who contribute unique value. I've also learned to practice the art of choice. This has been a key factor in my overall success.

The Power of Choice

The important piece to remember is that you have the ability to overwrite codes if you choose. There is power in choice, and you have to allow yourself to exercise this power. Even when others resist your way of thinking, recognizing that you have choices gives you more power.

Making choices helps shift your perceptions, and shifting your perceptions will help you make different choices.

You can begin by trying on different perspectives with a curious mindset and start changing experiences for yourself. This means putting away blaming and projecting problems onto other people, even if it really is their fault.

You will be better served by shifting from seeing obstacles to looking within yourself for opportunities to learn. You will need a strong desire and motivation to move beyond how you've been operating over the years. This experience will give you a healthier way of existing and will garner the composed soul that you desire.

Is this something you *want* to do?

Up to this very moment, you've done what you know to do. Now it's time to understand your natural algorithm and maximize it through this remodel of yourself.

Is this something you are *willing* to do?

Notice that I didn't ask you if you *can* do this. I know you can because you live in choice. If you choose to answer yes to these questions, then you are ready to move forward with your personal remodeling project.

Looking for Clues about Your Written Code through Stories

Start paying attention to stories. When you make a decision to remodel yourself, you subconsciously tune into those things that support your change. A great way to understand written code is to listen for it as you are talking to others. When you hear other people's stories, it gives you something to relate to or to recognize differences. You've probably noticed that I am using stories in this book, and you see bits and pieces of yourself in some of them. You are tuning into those things that look familiar to you, and can support your personal remodel. Speaking of stories, here's a good one.

STORY: Grandma Frankie's Influence on Aaron's Written Code

One morning, the hubby and I engaged in a deep conversation about natural algorithms as we sipped our morning coffee. He explains this next point so beautifully, and it needs very little wordsmithing to make sense.

It starts with a discussion about one of his core values, *knowledge*. Aaron is driven by research, so in his off time, he combs over different sources of information. I ask him what his underlying motivator is.

"My Grandma Frankie was always sharing information. She got me started on learning about new things. Back in the 70's, there were very few sources of information. You had *ABC News* on the television, which was the primary source available at that time. If you wanted to go deeper, you watched

60 Minutes or one of the few investigative shows to get a different perspective."

I silently recognize this experience as a pre-existing condition for Aaron. I ask, "So you gather information. How do you use it to achieve something?"

He says, "I don't need information to get a result, I just want to learn. I like to have information."

This is part of his written code and the way his brain is wired. It's a different perspective for me because I like to research things, but for other reasons. I need information to achieve a result. Interesting contrast. I dig deeper.

I ask, "How does that help you?"

"It fulfills my need to have facts and details (written code). When I was growing up, I was living in a world with very few sources of information. This gap left it wide open for people to operate too broadly and conceptually in their interpretation of how life should be. Rules were justified with "because that's just the way it is," and that impacted the course of my life." (Pre-existing condition.)

I see Aaron's viewpoint that being overly idealistic or conceptual can make things fuzzy, so facts, details, and rules are needed. When you don't know these three things, you are unsure as to how to interpret them. When someone is in authority and interprets them differently, you come out looking like the bad guy or the rebellious one.

We discuss the fact that detailed information and concepts are designed to support each other in a balanced relationship. If concepts grossly outweigh details, it's easier to manipulate any given situation. I'm choosing to take on a curious mindset right now, and my thoughts go to the Guyana tragedy. I look back for a moment.

Jim Jones was a self-made cult leader who was highly idealistic. He conjured up a possibility that a nuclear holocaust was imminent and led over 900 people to their death. How did he do it? He limited their sources of information. He isolated them from society, becoming the only authority and sole source of their needs. In his case, the scales were overburdened by concepts that had not been tested, proven, or validated. Instead, they were acted upon as law without supporting facts.

I take a moment to consider the flip side of this thought, where I tend to play more comfortably in the realm of concepts, patterns, and theory. We simply would not go forward as a society if we solely relied upon historical data, facts, or science to plunge us into the future. Most of these things point backward. When a new situation arises, and there's no data to back it, we can't fully rely on historical data to predict the future. I look to another moment for information. A Kodak moment.

Kodak was *a sad example of an organizational society who kept repeating what they always did—focus on film, printing pictures, and creating cameras. Contrary to popular belief, Kodak didn't fail because of their inability to embrace the digital age. In fact, they were at the forefront of it and invested in digital camera technology. They failed because they could not **envision** a transition from printing to online photo sharing. As the camera morphed into cell phones, printing photos died in the business world, along with its cumbersome processes and waste of tangible materials. (Scott Anthony, Kodak's downfall wasn't about technology; Harvard Business Review, July, 2016.) Had it not been for visualizing* *concepts and ideas, we would not have iPhones, wireless selfie sticks, or Facetime.*

I come back to the present conversation. I have a new perspective about his "written code." His brain wiring, combined with his life experiences and pre-existing conditions, help me to understand where he is coming from. I can see where these things manifest themselves in our marriage. I now understand why he needs detail, why he loves learning, and what makes him uneasy.

His pre-existing conditions center around the decisions that were being made around him as a child and were without substance, and it had a negative impact on him. Grandma Frankie was a catalyst for resource-finding and information, which aligned with the way his brain processed things. This helped him to develop his natural algorithm.

The value in our discussion heightens my awareness of how and why he responds the way he does, which gives me a better chance of composing my soul and not taking his reactions personally because I understand his natural algorithm.

Right now, I am trying to get clear on my own written code. Here's what I take away for my personal remodel in the conversation:

- I value knowledge and researching so I can put it to use and achieve things, which is a different motivator compared to my husband.
- I prefer to think big picture, so I bypass detail to get to the big picture. I don't ignore detail, I just go to it last.
- I recall stories and metaphors to help me process my understanding of something.

There's more, but this is enough detail so you can see how the examination of written code unfolds. You have probably realized that I also like to put things into three points. It's part of my written code—to get to the bottom line and simplify.

What Overwriting Code Looks Like

"Curiosity doesn't kill cats or people. Doing the same thing over and over without any strategy of improvement does. Just ask Kodak." -Angie Nuttle

Overwriting code is not a perfect science, and there is some artistry involved. Try on some different ways of processing data and new behaviors to see if they fit. Sometimes they do, sometimes they don't, but there's value in every effort you make to tweak your brain. Trying on new behaviors might be as simple as writing with your left hand instead of your right hand. If you are used to going to bed late, see what it's like to go to bed early. How about the act of remaining quiet instead of taking over the conversation with your spouse?

The sky's the limit regarding changing your routines and habits. This is part of the process to help you compose your soul. It's so easy to look at others and evaluate them, but it's less clear when you need to see yourself. Go deep, look at who you really are, no matter if it is attractive or scary. Stretching yourself helps you to overwrite codes that may not be serving you well or codes that need to become more refined.

STORY: The Wake-Up Call

I am good at what I do, and I am not ashamed to say it. Before becoming my own boss at Corporate Talent Institute, I worked in corporate America doing what I do now.

The problem is that I have historically thrown myself into the work, slathering in it, drowning myself in it with little room for anything else. I attribute my style to my extrovertedness combined with my intuitive-thinking way of processing things spontaneously. I can create visions and plans for hours and hours without getting tired.

My husband's complaints shed light on the problem. I was definitely on the hamster wheel of work, cranking it out, and moving up the ranks of success. The more I did, the more my employers demanded of my time. At one point I was traveling 70% of the time. The hubby was concerned.

I told myself I was building great leaders for the company, developing key talent, and pushing radical change programs because I wanted to be a part of something bigger than myself. When I look back and analyze what was going on, I see clearly that I was also masking deeper seeded emotional needs around acceptance and being needed. I had a need to be validated thanks to some pre-existing conditions, and work provided that for me. I was successful and recognized, but it was never enough for me.

It was an addiction to success and being validated. I needed to hear that I was valuable. I needed a fix every so often so that I could feel worthy enough. The organizations I worked for supported my habit with open arms because they reaped the benefits of my efforts.

I was also fighting the addiction of *doing*. A thought would enter my mind, and my brain directed me to activate it into an achievement. This frequent transaction was a product of my written code, and I was also enamored with the feeling it gave me. My reputation was one of creativity, quickness, pulling off impossible deadlines, and delivering stellar solutions. My style was one that was highly driven, and it landed me even more responsibility as a leader.

Work became a crutch whenever I didn't want to deal with issues at home. It was my hiding place, my refuge. If I was struggling with something, I would immerse myself in work. If I was going through a rough time, I would book an extra day on my business trip away from home. It became ridiculous.

One evening, I was sitting with a group of frontline leaders in Surrey, a small suburb in the UK of England. I had just completed a leadership development program with them, and everyone was talking about their experience. Drinks were flowing, guards were down, and it seemed like there was a sense of camaraderie. I was relishing in it, giving people last minute coaching as they asked their last questions before we departed. My extroverted brain was fed.

As they left, I was sitting there, and it struck me: "You can't keep doing this." I felt a sudden emptiness. Deep inside, I knew I needed to break this addiction. I was tired of the stress, the drowning myself in wine, the unhealthy cycle of traveling and never being fully present with my family. I hit a wall, and I knew that I couldn't sustain this path.

It was time to figure out what I really wanted and how I could shift from pressure to some sense of peace. I wasn't sure why I had a work addiction at that time, but it was there.

I would like to say, "One day I woke up and realized I needed to change my addiction to work, so I did and lived happily ever after." Well, I found out it doesn't work that way.

Changing deeply ingrained behaviors and mindsets take significant reconditioning and retraining. You learn in your journey that you have to try new things on, just like a shopping trip. You have to see if they fit. If things don't fit, you move on to something else until you find the right outfit for yourself.

STORY: Over-Productivity and Family Balance Experiment

I created a term for myself and people like me: The Overly Productive Person (OPP). Being overly productive is a result of written coding reinforced by pre-existing conditions.

The Overly Productive Person:

- Constantly works
- Constantly thinks
- Is rarely satisfied
- Rarely stops to rest

I recently attempted to make drastic changes to my OPP work habits so that I could be more present with my family. Anyone who owns your own business knows that when you move out of the corporate world, you don't really cut back the time you work, you just choose how you are going to shift those hours into other places. You probably also know that when you leave corporate, the corporate doesn't necessarily leave you. It's traumatic to make those changes if you try to do it all at once.

After several big discussions with my husband, I decided to try on a few new behaviors to address my work habits:

- I would work from 9 to 5, Monday through Thursday, and 9 to 3 on Fridays (you entrepreneurs might be laughing at this right now, it's okay).
- After 5 p.m., I would refrain from electronics to be more present and in tune with the family.
- I would work on getting away from the house and doing more activities like bowling, ball games, and movies.

For two weeks, I worked hard to implement the plan. I was determined, but immediately felt the pain of trying to squeeze the work into my new restrictive schedule. It just so happened that I had numerous deliverables and some difficult challenges happening on one of my big contracts that required significant time. This was going to be interesting.

Even so, I tried to make it work. The whole time, I was thinking, *This is not me.* Let's check in with my recollection:

The evenings without electronics and working start off okay. We interact a couple of times and play games, but I find that everyone transitions back to their electronics.

I tell myself, "Ang, you are doing this to give yourself a break."

The truth is that I find myself a bit resentful because I am trying to quit, and everyone else is still engrossed in those little tiny screens. That leaves me with trying to watch TV, and it doesn't last long. My value of doing things that are productive and yield some kind of fruit is screaming at me like a flared-up hemorrhoid.

It's saying, "Do something productive and meaningful!"

My answer is to find a quiet place and think. I visit the sunroom on a rainy night with the windows open. I sit out on the front porch around the beautiful flower garden that my mother has planted. I play with the dogs. I seek solace in the unspoken and quiet things.

I plan some *out of the house* activities like a shopping trip for me and Mackenzie, a trip to the bookstore, going out to dinner . . . anything that gets me away from the temptation to answer a few emails. The most worthwhile effort of everything I've done is the ou*t of the house activities.* It works well for me.

In the mornings, I take Mackenzie to school, rush to my office, and hit the ground running. I am literally running to and from bathroom breaks and taking a 5-minute lunch so I can fit everything in. At one point, I consider investing in Depends adult diapers so I can get the work done without any interruptions. I decided that is going too far. I'm smothering to death because I don't have the space to be at the level of creativity I need to be successful. I am trapped by structure. 9 to 5? Ridiculous goal.

I come close to breaking down emotionally one day as I'm rushing from a meeting to pick up the dogs from the groomer, and I get a speeding ticket. This is the first ticket I have gotten in 15 years. At first, I am angry and defensive, but I quickly humble myself because I deserve it. I was speeding. This is God's way of telling me it is time to slow down.

After two weeks, I find myself stressed, exasperated, and exhausted. I'm having nightmares almost every evening and wake myself up talking or shouting in my sleep. My work is slipping, and I am missing important details that I need to be paying attention to. I can't fit it all in, so I probably need to cut some of the work out. That means less money coming in.

One night, I unleash my desperation upon the family. I let them know I just can't squeeze everything in that needs to be done and meet all of their expectations. I'm frustrated and feel out of control. I go to bed at 7 p.m.

The next day, I review. Most things I am attempting do not coincide with my natural algorithm. However, I admit that I have accomplished four things in this experiment:

- I offloaded some of my tasks to my team members (although it had some price tags).
- I gained a coping mechanism of outside activity planning.

- I gained an appreciation and realized the value in taking time to sit and be mindful in peaceful places.
- Going to the gym actually helped me to experience some breakthrough thinking.

I also begin to learn two things:

1. I need to change out some yucky feeling words for something more positive:
   - From *have to* to *like to*
   - From *rules* to *decisions*
   - From *can't* to *choose not to*

2. I've gotten away from my personal mission and have been cooping myself up in my office. Heck, I am an extrovert! What am I doing sitting in my office all the time? The learning about my personal mission is eye opening, and I recognize that I need to get back on track.

My mission is to break people out of the invisible prisons they create for themselves, help them to get free, encourage them, and coach them to live their own missions. I want to show them that they have the ability to change their circumstances. I want to free them from self-imposed oppression. I want them to find the joy that I have found. I want people to believe that personal self-imprisonment is real. I want to be there when they realize their freedom and need help opening the prison door for themselves.

In remembering my defined mission, I recognize that I am actually in my own personal prison. I'm not connecting with people, and it's taking away my energy as an extrovert. I confirm this when I go to be onsite with a client and come away energized. I miss people and interacting with them. How did this happen?

I also realize that I haven't been making the decisions I need to. My values of responsibility and rescuing people have been clouding my vision when I need to call on logic and smart decision-making where staffing is concerned. I also get a chance to look at some big projects coming up that would take more time and energy to build upon, and I already have too many irons in the fire.

I have a revelation that I am operating contrary to my mission. Authenticity is extremely important to me, so I need to hit my reset button. I immediately recalibrate expectations with my team on some things so we could be more intentional and realistic. I also start getting people back on my calendar instead of planning so many isolated days in my office. I am starting to breathe easier now.

The Two Things That Impact a Successful Outcome

Later, as I revisited the situation and went deeper, I saw that beliefs played a big part in what changes stuck. For example, I didn't believe that getting off my electronics was going to change my relationship with my family. However, I did believe that getting off of my electronics would allow me to experience a good mental break so I could refresh myself and be more efficient. I didn't believe that the work was going to magically go away, but I did believe that I needed to take another look at prioritizing my work so I could be more present with the family.

The reality is that my beliefs and written code impacted my actions. I had to come face to face with the truth about me, who I am, and who I am not. The truth is that I like being overly productive and operate better when I have work to do.

I get validation by doing things for other people. I am not patient. I feel safer doing everything myself. I struggle to trust people to do what they say they are going to do.

There's more, but you see where I am going. I'm encouraging you to get clear on who you are, who you are not, and the truth about you. This self-discovery exercise will help you to accurately self-assess so you can properly compose your soul. You will also want to ask yourself good questions in every situation, like *why am I behaving this way and how do I become more aligned with my Natural Algorithm?*

How to Understand and Start Assessing Your Written Code

"Pause. Relax. Reflect. Three scary words to the Overly Productive Person." -Angie Nuttle

Everyone wants a solution to problems. To get to that place, you have to take the time to do a deep dive awareness. This is hard, especially for overly productive people because we want to pick up quick answers, so we don't lose our momentum.

Do you want to compose your soul? Then there is significant value in stopping to explore your natural algorithm. When you do this, you gain momentum for a sustainable result in your life.

There are several ways to approach this exercise, but the first goal is to take a 7-day inventory of what's true about you, who you are, and who you are not. You can start with an initial brainstorm to capture the immediate things that come to mind. Be sure to write down your thoughts and have some time to reflect on them.

I've designed some interesting and creative questions for you to work on. Some are straight and to the point; others are more conceptual and metaphorical. Don't try to do these all in one sitting because you find yourself checking the box. Box checking is a classic coping mechanism for overly productive people. Resist checking the box! Instead, **soak!** I know adding two exclamation marks is a writing no-no, but I'm choosing to emphasize heavily the importance of doing this exercise properly.

Exercise: The 7-Day Inventory

So, work on one section at a time, no more than one section a day for seven days. Set aside a certain time each day to do this work and commit to yourself that you will do this. This might mean you will have to get up a little earlier or stay up a little later.

Day 1: Brainstorm on what fits you:
- Who are you? (I am . . .)
- If you could create a list of job titles for yourself, what titles would be on the list?
- What is true about you? (The truth about me is...)
- What do you always do? (I always . . .)

Day 2: Brainstorm on what doesn't fit you:
- Who are you not? (I'm not . . .)
- What is not true about you? (What's not true about me is . . .)
- What do you never do? (I never . . .)
- What are deal breakers for you? (I consider it a deal breaker when . . .)

Day 3: Brainstorm on what drives you:
- What are your have to's? (I have to . . .)
- What are your must haves? (I must have . . .)
- What energizes you? (I am energized by . . .)
- When do you show up at your best? (I show up at my best when . . .)

Day 4: Brainstorm on what repels or exhausts you:

- What do you dislike? (I don't like . . .)
- What sucks the energy out of you? (What sucks the energy out of me is . . .)
- What can you absolutely not stand? (I can't stand . . .)
- What do you fear? (I fear . . .)

Day 5: Brainstorm on what it's like to be you:

- What is it like to be in your shoes at work? (To be in my shoes at work is like . . .)
- What do you love about yourself? (What I love about myself is . . .)
- What do you wish you could change about yourself? (I wish I could change about myself because . . .)
- What is it like to live your life outside of work? (To live my life is like . . .)

Day 6: Brainstorm on what feedback you get from other people:

- What do people frequently say about you? (People say that I am . . .)
- What action words or nicknames have people used to describe you? (People describe me as . . .)
- What do you like about the feedback? (I like . . .)
- What troubles you about the feedback? (What troubles me about the feedback is . . .)

Day 7: Brainstorm on ways you tend to cope:
- What do you do that is healthy for you? (Some things I do to stay healthy are . . .)
- What do you do that is unhealthy for you? (Some things I do that aren't so healthy are . . .)
- What is your typical way of managing challenging situations? (I handle challenges by . . .)
- What is your method for thinking about decisions? (My way of thinking about and making decisions is . . .)

Whenever I pose these types of questions to people, I get asked, "Do you want me to answer based on my professional life or my personal life? If you have to ask me this question, it automatically tells me that you are not being authentically you in some area of your life. You are a whole person; you don't check your emotions at the office door. Chances are you are putting up a front to protect who you really are.

I call it squashing your authenticity. When you squash the real you, you exhaust yourself. When you are exhausted, you run out of gas and can't be effective for anyone, especially yourself.

If you see this happening in your life, examine it. Why *do* you change your natural state of being in one place? Are there pre-existing conditions there? Is an inner critic talking to you? These act as coping mechanisms and put a big dent in your ability to influence with authenticity.

The next step will help you to understand if you are going against your written code, or if you simply have an inner critic that is messing with you. These will be important factors to be aware of as you work to compose your soul.

Assessment Challenge: Complete the MBTI

Once you have walked through the 7-Day Inventory Exercise, I recommend that you complete the MBTI® Type II Assessment. You can do this at www.schoolofep.com/MBTI, where you will get a full interpretative report with in-depth analysis for $75. If you want a free assessment, you can do a Google search on MBTI, and there are a few assessments out there that can give you basic results. Completing this assessment will help you get more granular and customized on your type and how it shows up in your written code.

As you recall from an early chapter, there are four brain-related dichotomies (opposing forces), and your results will show that you have brain-related preferences in each dichotomy:

1. Gaining energy and charging up (Introversion or Extroversion)
2. Taking in information and processing it (Sensing or Intuition)
3. Coming to decisions on what you've experienced (Thinking or Feeling)
4. Expressing your decisions in our everyday environment (Judging or Perceiving)

When you put all four of these brain preferences together, it creates a *type*. There are 16 different type possibilities. My type is ENTP, which means I naturally show up with brain preferences for the following brain processes:

- Extroversion
- Intuition
- Thinking
- Perceiving

These preferences influence everything I do: the how, when, and why I do what I do. These same principles apply to you.

The beauty of the MBTI Step II Assessment is that it shows deep insights around your type. You can get clues on how the environment is influencing your ability to freely operate within your preferences. We call this your level of clarity. You can also see each dichotomy broken down into five characteristics, or *facets*. It gives you good detail about your personal characteristics and strengths.

You also get some bonus information, like:

- Key behaviors in six major areas that typically show up for you
- Key behaviors that typically don't show up for you
- How you can be more impactful when dealing with opposing types

Once you know your results, move onto the next exercise, *Apply* the *Why*. It's not a deal breaker if you don't take the assessment, but it is helpful.

Exercise: **Apply the Why**

This exercise is simple to explain, and more difficult to accomplish because you ask *why* after every response.

In the last two exercises, you created a story about yourself. You also learned that there were brain-related functions that influenced your story. We want to connect these two exercises by asking *why*.

When used correctly, *why* breaks through the myth that people automatically understand the reasoning behind something. Some experts recommend you ask five *why's,* but I find that annoying. Be patient with asking why and allow yourself time to process it. If you need to ask five *why's,* go for it, but feel good if you get through three of them.

It's time now to reflect on why your answers to the questions are what they are. In some cases, you will see that you have pre-existing conditions wrapped up in your responses. In many cases, you will learn that the catalyst for your responses originates from your brain wiring.

1. Review the answers to your 7-day Inventory exercises. Select one of your question responses that stand out to you. (Put a star by it in your journal so you can keep track of the progress you are making.)
2. You may want to have this discussion with a close friend or someone you trust. Give them the assignment of asking the *why's.* You will find that they will be a great support in most cases and have valuable observations that you may not be aware of.
3. Apply three Why's to each of your responses. With each question, ask:
    a. Why? (Speak it out loud to a friend or write it down.)
    b. Why? (Go deeper below the surface.)
    c. Why? (Get to the core of your response.)

You may need to slightly adjust by asking, "Why is that important to you?" or "Why does that bother you?" Just don't go crazy, like "Why would you make a bonehead move like that?" The goal is to ask curious *why's* instead of judging *why's*.

You will be surprised at the insights you glean from this exercise. Overly productive people like us, seem to gloss over the why and just do whatever it is that needs to be done. Not all the time, but most of the time.

Here's a simple example:

Question: What do you wish you could change about yourself?

Answer: I wish I could change my inner thighs. They have a glob of fat there that never seems to go away. They rub together when I walk, and I always have trouble fitting into smaller size pants because of them, and it bothers me. I could be a size 6 if it weren't for my tree trunk thighs.

> **#1 Why** does that bother you? I feel like people look at me and think, "Wow, she has big thighs. That's weird." I'm just self-conscious.
>
> **#2 Why?** I don't want people to look at me negatively. I want them to know the real me, not the woman with the tree trunk thighs. I have great ideas, and I want them to be heard.
>
> **#3 Why** is that important to you? Because I get energy from connecting with people when we talk about possibilities. I am a possibility thinker. I want to be valued for my ideas.

If you look at this example, it's easy to see that there is a pre-existing condition at work. The self-consciousness is probably coming from an experience that involved criticism, judgment, or comparison.

Written code can clearly be seen as well in two of the four MBTI dichotomies:

- Extroversion- I get energy when I am with people.
- Intuition- I like thinking in possibility and playing with ideas

Once you walk through this exercise, apply the 3 Why's process to your other question responses. I give you permission to select certain questions and leave other ones alone if you want. I do recommend that you come back to your responses periodically and run through this process. It's good medicine for your soul and gives you a sense of doing something that adds value.

Check In: Why Is This Important Again?

It's important to understand your written code and recognize it so you can know what composes your soul. When you operate within your preferences, life clicks together like the pieces of a puzzle. Everything aligns, and it just seems easier. You will also be alerted to what causes you to feel at odds with the world. You will see this, especially in an environment where you have to operate against your code.

Here is an example that relates to your job:

Your day-to-day job is on a production line running a piece of equipment alone all day long. You do the same thing over and over, never speaking to anyone except at the beginning and end of your shift. This is fantastic if you are introverted. It's also wonderful if you like structure (judging preference) and dealing with known concrete tasks that are the same all the time (sensing preference). You are aligned with your preferences in your written code.

Now imagine that you are an extrovert. You enjoy talking to people and sharing ideas (intuitive preference), and you also like spontaneous variety in your day (perceiving preference). You are going to hate that job. Depending on your financial circumstances, you will either quit as soon as you find a new job, or you will disengage completely for a while due to your complete boredom.

Then you will quit.

If you are working in a job you despise and you aren't doing what you do best, your soul is not going to be happy and content.

Working in a job or situation where you enjoy what you do is foundational. You probably spend most of your time working, so it's important to take on a curious mindset about your surroundings. You may dislike some things about the environment, the politics, or your boss. This is the real world, but it can be a phenomenal growth opportunity for you.

Your default brain wiring is going to always be there, but you can add some new paths to unused parts of your brain, which is a good thing. This is robust brain development.

Whenever I do workshops, I conduct an exercise where I have participants write their names five times with their dominant hand. Then I have them switch hands and write their name again. There's moaning, groaning, and laughing at this point. People are uncomfortable, but they do it.

We discuss the fact that if they keep practicing it, they will be able to get a better looking signature over time. The deeper science is that this wakes up a part of the brain that doesn't get activated often. When we activate more brain matter, we become more well-rounded in our thinking. This doesn't override our default brain wiring; it creates additional pathways that bring life and rejuvenation to our minds.

This same principle applies when you are in an environment that operates differently than you do. As long as you are doing what you love, you can grow and stretch, learning how to adapt to new situations. On the contrary, if you keep doing the same process year after year, your brain starts to shut down its doors. When you don't use it, you lose it.

CHAPTER 4

HOW TO POWER UP YOUR VALUES

"If you are feeling exhausted and you don't have energy at the end of the day, you are unplugged from your main power source: Your Values."
-Angie Nuttle

Where do values come from? You aren't exactly born with them, but they are developed as you go through life. I like to say they are the byproduct of your brain wiring and your pre-existing conditions.

We value lots of things.

I *value* my husband and children. I *value* vacations. I *value* my alone time. When I talk about *having values*, it takes on a different meaning. What I value taps into something deeper that gets to my real core values.

When I have alone time, I experience a sense of focus. When I spend time with my family, it gives me a sense of belonging. When I go on vacation, I gain crystal clear clarity. These are values that are important to me, and I align with them when I experience these situations.

Values are what is most important to you, no matter what situations are going on around you, no matter who is in front of you, and no matter what things are in your life. Values are the driving force of your actions and decisions. They evoke strong emotions, and they are always working inside you.

Take a moment to jot down what you think your values are. What are they? If you could name your top 5, what would you say? While you are thinking about that question, I'll give you an example of what a value looks like and how it shows up.

Value Example: Harmony

Let's say one of your values is *harmony*. It's interesting to note that the MBTI *Feeling* preference commonly fits this value. Feelers are wired to shy away from conflict. They choose to focus on the positive instead of the negative aspects of a situation. To maintain harmony, Feelers may see conflict as painful and even unnecessary.

Because harmony is important to you, you will look for ways to honor it in every situation. When you meet people, you will seek common ground with them. Your activities will revolve around creating more harmony. You might give people gifts. You might encourage people to look at the bright side of everything, or lead them to a peaceful solution. Your mantra is "We can all get along!"

When harmony is lacking, you quickly do what is necessary to get it back on track. You try to correct conflict and restore the good feelings that harmony evokes. If the conflict is too great, you may avoid that situation completely in order to maintain harmony within yourself. You may look for a new situation that honors your value. If you feel that you are trapped in a situation that opposes your value, you may shut down completely or leave that situation. This value alone drives people to leave their jobs, spouses, and end relationships.

A pre-existing condition can spark and amplify your value of harmony. This can come from either pleasant or unpleasant experiences.

- **Positive Experience**: You grew up with a family who sat together at dinner every night. Everyone was respectful of other's ideas, listened to each other, and laughed together. You loved the sense of harmony and peaceful acceptance, and now you look for ways to recreate it.
- **Negative Experience:** You felt the pain of an abusive father or mother. You learned that if you were quiet and smiled a lot, your parent wouldn't be so angry and all would be well. Now you look for ways to avoid these difficult scenarios.

Chances are that your value of harmony was nurtured by similar experiences. It's important to understand where it comes from so you can clarify, honor, and manage it in a healthy way.

The 2 Types of Values

Values are essential to your natural algorithm, much like your heart is essential to your body. Values carry life through your veins. You move to their rhythmic beat. They look for ways to be honored, recognized, and respected. They defend against potential threats. They drive your decisions. When you align with them, it's a perfectly consistent flow that cycles through your day. When you don't align, then the flow gets pinched off, and your natural algorithm suffers irregularity.

You have two kinds of values, and both evoke certain emotions:

- **Foundational:** These are the values that have to be in place for you to be stable, content, and functional. If your foundational values are missing or out of alignment, then you feel uncomfortable and even miserable when they are being stepped on.
- **Inspirational:** These values get you out of bed and can have you burning the midnight oil because you are so in love with them. Your inspirational values are your fuel for your personal mission. They get you beyond the day-to-day routine and into a more meaningful life when you align with them.

Let's look at the difference between these two in some examples.

I have a value around *order and cleanliness*. After a long day of working, I want to walk into a clean house free of clutter. I don't want to pick up trash, socks, or strewn clothes. I don't want to deal with dirty dishes on the counters and the sinks. When faced with this situation, I become annoyed and irritable. It is difficult to sit down in the midst of clutter and disorganization. Visions of that hoarder show on television dance in my head.

This is a foundational value in place for me. I am very uncomfortable when it gets stepped on or isn't being honored. I work hard to minimize the violations that are committed against this value so I can sit down, decompress, and honor some of my inspirational values, like fun and laughter.

I love to laugh and look for fun things that bring lightheartedness. Napoleon Dynamite is my go-to movie for quirky, clean humor. I look for things that I can laugh at heartily, like Snap Chat. This hysterical phone app allows you to send quick video messages and apply filters to your face.

I became obsessed with Snap Chat and was sharing little messages with everyone I knew (until they asked me to quit). I got some great laughs out of it with my family, even though they became a little annoyed by my overuse of it. Overall, it has created extra bonding in the family.

This inspirational value of laughter is driving me to look for ways to honor it. When I am aligning with it, I get more energy and joy. I want to share it with the world, and I can keep honoring this value until I pass out from exhaustion.

Exercise: Examining the Most Commonly Claimed Values of Family and Integrity

Most foundational coaching work starts with getting clear on your values. If you have never worked with a coach, values cultivation will be new and even feel a bit clunky to you. I want you to move away from just selecting values from a list because people tend to pick values they think they *should* have. We also tend to generalize or clump lots of values into one big one. Let's start by exploring the two most common values identified by people I meet:

FAMILY

I can't tell you how many times people identify *family* as their top value, but it appears to be absent in their day-to-day lives. They spend more time working, stalking their phones, searching social media, and connecting with everyone but their family.

This may describe you, and I want you to know there is no condemnation in this. You started a family for a reason, and it's related to what your true values are. The family is a result of those values coming into play. I want to challenge you to go deeper than just *family*. We want to look at what family *gives you*. This will help you to get clear on what is really driving you.

Take a moment to reflect and journal about these questions:

1. What is important to you about family?
2. What prompted you to have a family (or not have one)?
3. What does family give you?
4. What situation typically overrides time with your family?
5. For #4, what value are you most commonly honoring over time with your family?

When you answer these questions, it causes your more deeply ingrained values to surface, like commitment or responsibility. Write down what shows up for you.

INTEGRITY

Integrity rivals family in the top two most mentioned values of all time. In society, most people agree that integrity should be a cornerstone. It's broad definition warrants a distilling down of what it really represents for us. Try to get to the heart of what the deeper value is for you by checking out this definition.

If you look at the various definitions, integrity has three main parts. I love what Dictionary.com says:

- *The adherence to moral and ethical principles; soundness of moral character; honesty.*
- *The state of being whole, entire, or undiminished.*
- *A sound, unimpaired, or perfect condition.*

What an incredible way to articulate integrity. Who *doesn't* want to hold this as a value? To be perfect, whole, and honest is quite a state of being, and it sounds more like a goal to reach. The only way I know how to accomplish all these things is to be in a relationship with God since He is the one who makes us whole and perfect. Yet, we strive to get to that place of integrity, which prompts my next statement.

Something else is driving the need and desire for integrity. You could be gaining a sense of safety when you practice integrity by following the rules. You may be valuing transparency or honesty because you don't like being deceived and you need trust.

What is it for you? Take a moment to answer these questions:

1. What is important to you about integrity?
2. What prompts you to practice integrity?
3. What does integrity give you?
4. What situation typically overrides integrity?
5. For #4, what value are you most commonly honoring over integrity?

Reflect on this one for a few days. Look for evidence of how *integrity* is showing up for you, and what form it is taking. Is it showing up as *honesty*, *safety*, or something else?

Validate its existence and frequency in your life. Frequency is important. If it isn't there, then you are probably valuing something else instead. Identify your pattern and capture what you are truly valuing in your life.

Exercise: Distill and Refine Your Top 5 Values

I asked you to write down your top 5 values, and now it's time to evaluate them as I showed you for the values of *family* and *integrity*. Answer the five questions, filling in the blank with each one of the values you identified:

1. What is important to you about _____?
2. What prompts you to practice _____?
3. What does _____ give you?
4. What situation typically overrides _____?
5. For #4, what value are you most commonly honoring over _____?

If you are struggling with coming up with your values, a great way to create your list is to look at what you do on a daily basis. You tend to do what is important to you. You can also look more closely at what makes you get an extra oomph of emotion. Use the five evaluative questions to distill your activities down to values.

The good news is that you've laid the groundwork for yourself in the 7-Day Exercise, and the 3 Why's Exercise. Your values will surface through those exercises. Go back to the questions I asked and scan them for themes in the following areas:

1. Based on your exercises and reflections, what is important to you?
2. What stands out in your answers? What do they point to?
3. What situation compels you emotionally, and what does it trigger for you?
4. What do you *always* do, no matter what? What value are you honoring as a result?

5. What do you *never* do, no matter what? What value are you honoring as a result?

This is a valuable exercise to come back and review on a regular basis. When we are faced with a year's worth of ups, downs, and changes; reconnecting with your values will give you fuel. You will also have a chance to gain new insights on how you are aligning with your values, and where you can improve.

I want to give you permission to name your values whatever you want. You don't have to have the traditional names like authenticity or responsibility, although you can certainly claim those as your own. For example, I have a name for my values of clarity and focus—*Crystal Clear*. She is present every day in my life. I seek her out when I deal with a client or try to understand someone's perspective.

If you have a value around creativity, you will get to practice it in the next chapter by creatively naming your values, along with your inner critics.

CHAPTER 5

MEET YOUR INNER COMMITTEE

"Everybody wants to be the boss. We just don't want to be responsible for the results if something goes wrong." -Angie Nuttle

You have an inner committee. This committee acts as an executive board or a command center for every decision you make.

You have members on your committee that hold certain values, pre-existing conditions, and written code as sacred. They act as lobbyists who try to influence what you do, and how you go about it. Each member has an area of experience and adds unique value. For example, you have a member who values safety and regulates danger for you (we will name this member *Dr. Danger for the purpose of this explanation*). When you are driving, and someone is running a red light when you are trying to turn, Dr. Danger moves into the executive decision-making seat and tells you, "STOP! That car is running a red light and will hit you!" Of course, you are going to listen because you don't want to end up in the hospital or in a coffin.

You might have another committee member who values having fun. Let's say that when you think of fun, you picture a party with balloons and confetti, so you call this member, *Party Time*. You decide it's time to take a vacation so you can relax and have fun, so *Party Time* naturally steps up and helps you decide where to go and what to do.

But what happens when these two get crisscrossed, and one committee member is dominating the decisions? What if *Party Time* is the decision-maker when that car is running the red light? Or *Dr. Danger* keeps butting in when you are trying to go on vacation? It can spell disaster and misalignment, which leaves you feeling dissatisfied and miserable.

Envision your inner committee in the business world. You are at work, and *Party Time* shows up during a serious meeting, and you end up losing credibility because you didn't bring forth the right committee member. This happens more often than you think because we allow certain members to take over our decisions, get us stuck in a rut, and we don't progress.

There are a few things that have to be understood regarding your personal values and their presence on your inner committee, so here is a recap:

- Clarity on what your real values are is critical to managing them.
- Your personal values guide your decisions and your life (just in case you forgot).
- You may be misaligned with your values, and you know it because you are stressed, exhausted, and stifled most of the time.
- To have a composed soul, values alignment is critical.

As we start working on your inner committee, there are a few things to realize:

- Your most important values have a seat at the table.
- They are responsible for where you are today.
- Your committee members all want to be in the executive seat.
- You also have inner critics that sit on your committee (we will address these annoying voices later).
- You have the power to reset this inner committee and decide who is going to be on it, and who needs to sit down and be quiet.

One of the best ways to recognize who's on your inner committee is to think about the stories of your day-to-day interactions. Specifically, identify the decisions you are making in those stories, and *who shows up*. I shared one of my committee members with you already: *Crystal Clear*. She appears when I need more information or I want to analyze a situation.

There are others who show up too, and they originate from my pool of values. Here are a few examples, along with some of the creative names I've come up for them:

1. **Madam CEO:** She is my confident executive leader who takes command of the room and doesn't waver in her decisions. She takes direction from God. She values *action*, *competence*, and *confidence*.
2. **Fully Present:** She is the intent listener who wants people to feel valued and appreciated. She values *appreciation*, *acceptance*, and *having a voice*.
3. **Crisis Manager:** She takes over when there is a challenge or crisis, sees the big picture, and restores

order quickly. She reassures all that everything is going to be okay. She is the survivor, the responsive one who helps people feel secure. She values *reassurance, responsiveness,* and *restoration.*

4. **Executive Coach:** She is my conflict resolver who can put her feelings in neutral while helping others. Executive Coach is the calm force, and in the eye of the hurricane can navigate through the damaging winds. She helps people come to agreement. She values *composure, peace,* and *living in choice.*

I'm going to give you a chance to name your own committee members at the end of this chapter, so be thinking about who they might be. First, I want to demonstrate how committee members strive for the executive seat and can end up in the wrong seat at the wrong time.

STORY: When the Wrong Committee Member Gets in the Driver's Seat

It was June 27, 2006.

I had been in Iraq for over two years working as a Human Resources defense contractor. Life was going pretty well from my perspective, and it seemed like my vision of success was coming together. I was experiencing a series of career successes, and it felt good to be recognized for my work. Promotions into leadership came, which confirmed that I was finally doing something right.

While working there, I was able to pay off some serious debt I accumulated as a college student and single parent. I was finally able to provide my kids-financial stability and even saved some money for their college funds. This was a far cry from a few years prior when we were walking around the Wal-

Mart parking lot looking for change to pay for a $3.00 school function.

I got a bonus blessing in Iraq because I met my future husband, who was also a defense contractor and site manager.

Yep, things seemed to be going well, until June 27, 2006.

I was busy. As a matter of fact, I had been busy for several months working 12-14 hour shifts every single day. But, I wasn't that tired. I was energized by the work, by being respected, and being a part of something bigger. I was in my element of living in a responsive environment. I fed off the crisis and chaos to the point that I didn't have much time for anything else. Or anyone else.

Crisis Manager was in charge of my inner committee a good portion of the time in Iraq. Here's my most impactful recollection during that time:

As I walk into my makeshift office this particular morning, I notice that it is unusually quiet. I sit down, sip my coffee, and turn on my computer. The phone rings, and it is my sister, Natalia.

"Hey Sister! How's it going?" I gleefully spout.

"I have some news." Her tone is solemn and strange.

"Okay, what's up?" I figure she's going to share some gossip or relationship news.

"Mom is very sick. She's been diagnosed with leukemia." She sounds a bit weepy.

"Oh no! That's terrible!" I have a wave of emotion and surprise but feel hopeful.

"That's not all." She says with a building drama in her voice. *I wonder how Dad is taking it.*

"Dad was on his way to be with Mom after she got the news, and he was in a car accident." I'm thinking, *Oh Lord, Mom's sick and Dad is in the hospital.*

"He didn't make it."

BOOM.

Did I hear that correctly? My dad didn't make it? How can this be? I just spoke to him a few days earlier on Father's Day. This has to be a mistake! Is my dad gone? Is this a joke? What is happening?

"He was on his way home on his usual route, he was turning, and someone ran a red light. They hit him hard. He died instantly."

SHOCK.

Lightning runs through my whole body. I literally feel and see a bright flash in my head. Trying to hold myself together and calm my sudden gasp for air, I give my sister instructions to get a Red Cross message sent over so I can leave the Mosul base and get back to the states. I barely remember anything at that moment. I go out into the hallway and cry out.

My coworkers run out to comfort me, and just take over the situation. They make all my arrangements as I grieve in the moment.

I am the picture of uncomposed. My soul reels in deep pain and trauma. A sense of palpable guilt and shame sets in as I think back to our last conversation together on Father's Day.

"Hey Ang, it's your dad!"

"Hey Dad, I was about to call you. Happy Father's Day!"

"Thanks, sweetie. I just called to tell you that I love you the mostest!"

"I love you too, Dad. How are you feeling these days?" I'm halfway listening because I'm busy monitoring my computer for incoming HR problems.

"I'm tired." He's speaking in his baby voice, like he did when I was a kid. I'm amazed at his jovial spirit; he's been diagnosed with Parkinson's at 57 years old and has finally decided to retire.

"Well, I love you. Hey Dad, can I call you back later? Something's just come in, and I need to take care of it." My attention is now fully focused on a brewing employee relations issue that I need to deal with.

"Okay, sweetie. I love you the mostest."

"Love you too. Bye."

I don't realize I would be saying bye forever.

As I get on the plane at our base in Mosul, I keep replaying our conversation over and over in my head.

If I would have just stayed on the phone longer . . .
If I would have just been fully present with him . . .
If I would have just shut off my computer . . .
If I would have only realized this would be the last time . . .

As I look back at that moment, I see that *Crisis Manager* was busy controlling my decisions. I quieted the voices of some of my other important committee members, like *Fully Present*. An inner critic was beating the hell out of me emotionally, condemning me for my lack of committee management. *Madam CEO* was nowhere to be found. She went offline, incapacitated and grieving heavily after being stun-gunned with the traumatic news.

Valuable time was lost with my father because I was too busy looking for the next problem, the next opportunity. I was looking to be needed and feel important when I was actually needed by my dad at that moment.

He was the person who saw me as important, and I missed seeing it. I failed to be fully present with him, and I minimized an opportunity to experience joy with him. *Crisis Manager* was misplaced, and there was no way to sugar coat the situation to make it better.

I wasn't there for him, and that's it.

Looking back at that situation teaches me so much about my inner committee. Eventually, *Madam CEO* recovered, took over, and helped me to move forward. It's like my whole committee came together after that and had a series of meetings that made new rules for me. I am still working to fully implement them, but I'm in a better place today than I have been in a long time.

Crisis Manager occasionally pops into the executive chair and has to be kicked out, but my self-awareness has increased, and I know when to call forth *Madam CEO* or another member.

Exercise: Discover Your Inner Committee Members

Composing your soul includes the ability to lead and manage your inner committee in a way that serves you well. Let's get on the path to learning who's on it so you can start to maximize the relationship with your members.

If you notice in my committee member descriptions, some values tend to bind together to form a theme or a character. The process of identifying your committee members is not prescriptive. Don't think you have to have three set values to do this. You can start with one of your top 5 values and process how it shows up in your world. Later, you may see how some of your values pop up and support or join forces with others.

Over the next week, reflect on these questions in your journal, or talk through them with a friend:

1. Think of a story where you had to make a major decision. Process the whole story:
    - What was the general situation?
    - What was the challenge or conflict?
    - What was the result or outcome?
    - What did you realize?

2. Identify the values that showed up for you in the story:
    - What emotions were you experiencing?
    - How did you behave?
    - What actions did you take?
    - What values materialized for you?

3. Characterize the values with a name or *persona:*
    - Is there a theme that surfaces for you about these values?
    - What's the first name that comes to mind?
    - Is there a TV or movie character that comes to mind?
    - Is there a metaphor you can apply?

On step 3, you will want to process the questions and then decide on one name or character for each member. Don't make it complicated or overthink it, just go with what flows and fits. Most of the time, the first thing that pops into your head is the answer.

1. Once you identify a character, add it to a list you create in your journal, called *Inner Committee*. Move on to another story and process the three steps again.

2. When you have identified a few committee members, do a quick scrub test by comparing it to your list of top 5 values:
   - How are your top 5 showing up on your board?
   - What's missing?
   - What's new or different?

If something is missing or different, it tells me that you may have identified a value that isn't one of your top 5. You don't have to scramble to make it fit, just notice and let it exist. You have other values that are more of a priority, which is fine. Allow yourself to be self-aware and just receive it.

The important takeaway here is to recognize the drivers behind your decisions. When you understand the way you process your written code, you begin to realize that you are the boss of your inner committee. You aren't a victim anymore.

But wait.

There is another voice talking to you and influencing your life. It's your inner critic, and it's one of the enemies of a composed soul. We will examine this formidable opponent in the next chapter.

CHAPTER 6

THE INNER CRITICS

"I've learned that it's more important to be effective versus perfective. If everyone would stop criticizing me, everything would be perfect."
-Angie Nuttle

"You should have let out the dogs already."

My husband mutters under his breath as he heads downstairs one Saturday morning.

It is 6:00 a.m. I am sitting in the loft area of my house enjoying my quiet time, which is a part of my daily "compose your soul" routine. My logic is to get up early, talk to God, and journal, then let the dogs out.

I attempt to explain my rationale but obviously didn't get the reaction I was hoping for.

Buddy and Jovie, my two Havanese dogs, have a habit of digging holes in the yard and coming back inside like dirty hot messes. Since the hubby had bathed them the night before, I want to preserve their cleanliness to avoid tracking it in the house while preserving his sense of accomplishment.

I experience an avalanche of raw thoughts and feelings in the moment. A voice appears in my head and triggers some of my personal hot buttons. The voice is my inner critic, the character who points out all of my flaws, inadequacies, and shamefulness.

I'm going to semi-pause this story to educate you about the voice of the inner critic. This includes a quick characterization of what I was processing in my head during this interaction with the hubby:

1. **"Should-itis" or "Should-Ann":** *The feeling you get when you or another person imposes judgment, and it leads to inflammatory guilt. You should do this, or I should do it that way.* The only thing I was hearing was the hubby "should-ing" all over me. (I have to note here that I borrowed this phrase from my friend and colleague, Gretchen, who shared it during a ladies day session we attended together. Thanks, Gretchen!) I sometimes call this inner critic "Should-Ann" because it reminds me of an overbearing and gruff woman who bosses people around. Her weapons of choice are shame and condemnation.

2. **"You didn't do it right":** *You have a feeling of imperfection or inadequacy, so obviously you aren't good enough or smart enough.* I immediately went here, questioning myself as to why I didn't choose a different approach. Of course, I was a little merciful to myself on this one because I made my decision *before* I had coffee.

3. **"You caused a conflict":** *You observe the other person's reaction, and you take responsibility for their feelings and behaviors.* If I had only said it *this* way, or if I had just let the dogs out, the hubby wouldn't have been upset. Instinctively I knew that was not true; he would have been upset either way. For some reason, I thought I could control his feelings and blamed

myself for his reaction and the perceived lack of harmonious dialogue.

4. **"Who made you the boss?":** *You become defensive. You think of all the bad things the other person has ever done or said, then throw it into a big boiling pot of blame.* When the hubby got a case of the "should-itis" on me, my memory bank magically produced of all the things he did wrong in the past (leaving trash around, tracking mud through the house, etc.).

5. **"I'm never being considerate of you again, jerk face!":** *After reviewing reruns of your life and lessons learned while you compare them to the situation at hand, you resolve never to do or say certain things again. You do this to teach the other person a lesson, or even get back at them. Except, the only person it hurts is you.* I found myself going down a rabbit hole of anger, vowing to never go out of my way to be thoughtful again. A physical reaction was happening in my body—a tight and tense feeling in my shoulders, chest, and jaw.

These five reactions worked in my head and created an emotional cocktail because of one statement, "You should have let the dogs out already." I was taking this whole situation out of context. I was also taking on the emotions belonging to another person and claiming responsibility for his behavior.

I was letting someone's words and tone have power over me because of the story my inner critic was telling me. I started the day with good intentions and was ironically in the middle of a bible study. I allowed a few unrequested words knock me totally off course.

Now let's come back to the story.

After stewing for a few minutes, an inner committee member steps up to the table—*Executive Coach*. She reminds me that I have to live consistently with how I coach other people who are faced with similar situations. A barrage of new and different thoughts emerge for me.

- I don't control other people; I can only control myself (but I can influence them).
- My way of doing things may be different than others' ways.
- I'm not responsible for someone else's reactions, behaviors, and emotions.
- People show up based on what is working inside of them.
- I don't have to live in a world of should-itis; I live in a world of choice.

Executive Coach reminds me that the enemy is not my husband; it is my inner critic. This calms me. She decides to take over the discussion with the hubby.

Later, my hubby comes back to me and sits down. I share with him that our early morning interaction is a great inspiration for my book.

"Oh yeah? Tell me more."

As I tell my introverted and severely private sweetheart about my writings, his facial expression shifts from skepticism to surprise. His eyes widen, and he reveals his thought. He mumbles something under his breath, processing what he was thinking but not making it clear to me.

You may be wondering what the misunderstanding is. I don't know the answer. The day is young, we are both waking up, and Aaron is hearing a voice in his head that caused him to react. All that matters is that a misinterpretation occurred, and we are dealing with the aftermath.

"It was a misunderstanding. I thought you said something else. I didn't hear you correctly."

Amazing. One misunderstanding evolves into a big emotional processing center in my head and leaves my husband going through his own train of thought. At the moment of dissension, he was dealing with an inner critic as well that instigated his defensiveness earlier.

The result is that it has caused me to capture myself dealing "in process" with an inner critic who is trying to make me feel yucky. It's a beautiful example of what happens in our minds when we encounter other people with our mental filters on, and our ears turned off.

The Scoop on Inner Critics and Where They Come From

Inner critics are adept at finding their way to the table of your inner committee. They act like viruses, spreading their germs like wildfire all throughout your written code. They interfere with your ability to see the facts of a situation clearly. They distort the natural way your brain is wired and try to create destructive neural pathways. They are also the culprits for getting you emotionally stuck so that you can't move forward in your mission.

Where do they come from?

Inner critics are born as a result of your pre-existing conditions. They formulate when you've had negative experiences that end in shame, guilt, or inadequacy. Here are eight common examples of inner critics. I've taken the liberty of giving them names:

1. **Perfectionist:** You must do everything right. If you miss one thing, then you are a failure.

2. **Imposter:** You don't deserve to be in the room because you don't know anything. These people are much smarter than you. You will be discovered and removed.

3. **Competency Police:** You must know everything, or you are incompetent. Dummy!

4. **Micro Manager:** You must control everything, or it will all fall apart, and the world will end. It will all be your fault.

5. **Excluder:** You don't fit. You are not wanted or needed. Nobody wants to talk to you here. Get out.

6. **Critical Parent:** You should have done (insert task). You should be ashamed of yourself.

7. **Martha/Mary** (from the bible): You're not enough, and you can't do enough. You have to keep producing and doing more stuff. Keep working and moving so you can show your value, and then criticize Mary because she's just sitting around.

8. **The Discourager:** You aren't going to succeed, so give it up. You should just stick with what you are comfortable with. Who do you think you are, trying to be someone better than everyone else?

I am sure you have versions of these characters and others. They've developed over the years and have refined their presence so that you just accept their word as truth. They pretend to operate according to your written code. But let me tell you, they do not speak the truth. Inner critics take a small granule of fact or a flat-out lie and blow it out of proportion.

Is it wrong to seek perfection or gain knowledge? Absolutely not. Seeking something good or better comes from a positive place of wanting to grow and improve. This is healthy and normal.

The inner critic doesn't function this way. Instead, its goal is to beat you up and put you in a personal prison.

Inner critics are never satisfied until they attach the shame, guilt, or inadequacy to everything. They are responsible for putting up stop signs at the places where you could potentially show up like a rock star. They can also guilt you into action, even though you don't want to do it. They disrupt your natural algorithm with their malware tendencies. Here are a couple of examples:

- **Stop Sign Tactic:** You are sitting in a meeting where the subject matter is important to you. You want to speak up and contribute, but the *Competency Police* arrests you. *What are you thinking? You don't know enough, and you certainly aren't intelligent enough to add any value. Stand down, stupid!"* You end up sitting there without saying a word.

- **Guilting Tactic:** A close family member wants you to co-sign on a loan for her daughter's college. You've co-signed on a loan before with the family member, and you ended up getting stuck with the payments. You've also loaned that person money and never got it back. The family member desperately claims that if you don't sign, her daughter won't go to college. *Critical Parent* shows up and loads you with a dose of "should-itis." *Now, you know you should co-sign. That poor child won't be able to go to college, and it will be all your fault. If you don't sign, you will be a disgrace to the family.*

Guess what? God wants his job back. It's not your job to take on every single person's burden. Your inner critic will gain even more power when you keep making the same mistake over and over. People see those kinds of weaknesses and vulnerability too and take advantage of them. Is it wrong? Yes. But, you have the power to shut down that inner critic. If you choose not to, then it's on you.

*My side note is this: If you want to give, then give because God directs you to do it and because it brings you joy, expecting nothing in return. Otherwise, you are going to miserable.

I would say that your inner critics are at least 50% of your battle when you are pursuing a life of freedom, peace, and fulfillment. Become keenly aware of them because they are there. Some are more obvious than others.

Inner critics are not your friends, so, to compose your soul, let's stop playing with them.

Exercise: Identify Your Inner Critics

Work through the following questions in your journal, or discuss with a friend:

1. Review the eight types of inner critics I mentioned. Which ones do you recognize in your own life?
2. How do they show up for you? What kinds of situations are common?
3. Are there other types of inner critics that you recognize? Describe them.

Once you go through this initial exercise, list your inner critics and ensure that you title them properly based on how they show up. Again, there is no formula or science to this. Write down whatever pops up.

For example, let's say you have an inner critic who is constantly condemning you to hell or rebuking you somehow. You might get a picture of the *Church Lady* or *School Master*. Don't allow *Perfectionist* to come in and take you down a rabbit hole. Write it down and don't overthink it.

Your next step is to analyze each of your inner critics by reflecting upon the following questions:

1. What does this inner critic tell you about yourself?
2. What is the weapon it uses: shame, guilt, inadequacy, condemnation, or something else?
3. What emotional hot button is being triggered in you?
4. If you look back in your life, where was this inner critic born?

The last question is a big one that needs searching out and reflection by you. When I work through this with people, they identify some high-level generalization like: "I just had a strict parent" or something that minimizes the full impact of the experience. It's a good place to start but go deeper.

Identify specific experiences that truly influenced you. Instead of stepping into a place of blame, just *notice* what happened and how it impacted your thinking. Think about the emotions that surfaced for you then, and now.

Everything I'm sharing with you about inner critics leads to something I call the 5-Step Wash Cycle. It's a healthy way to shut down those annoying voices that are there to load you with guilt, shame, and inadequacy.

Tool: The 5-Step Wash Cycle to Get the Inner Critics Out

Being with an inner critic leaves you with sticky toxicity. It also leads you to develop some of those pre-existing conditions we talked about in an earlier chapter.

How do you get over the inner critic? You tell it to shut up because you are the boss of it, not vice versa. You do this purposely and consistently.

I use this 5-step process to overcome the inner critic attack and regain my composure. I like to think of it as if I am running the inner critic through the washing machine. I drop in the inner critic to let it soak, start the wash cycle, let it spin, do a final rinse, then dry and fold. The toxicity is washed away.

I don't want to leave you with a cliffhanger on the "You should have let the dogs out" story, so I will incorporate that example to show you the steps:

1. **Drop in and Soak.**

Be with the inner critic for a few minutes. I allowed myself to walk through the dark side of my thoughts after hearing my hubby's words. It's like letting a virus run its course.

There isn't much you can do about it in the moment except rest so that your body can recover faster. I explored all the places that the inner critic wanted to go, and let it wander, and I became an observer of it instead of a participant. I *noticed it*, then wrote about it in my journal, which helped tremendously.

2. **Start the Wash Cycle.**

Shift thinking to the light load. I made a conscious choice to "explore alternatives" and examine how the thinking was valuable to my personal learning. I decided to be curious and funnel that negative energy into something that I could productively use.

It takes a tremendous amount of energy and discipline to move from toxic thinking to curious inquiry, and I can say that I have gotten pretty good at it over the last few years. Ask yourself questions like, *how is this comical?* Or *what is good to know for future reference?*

3. **Let it Spin.**

Squeeze out the toxicity. I began to release my negative state of mind by speaking about it. I shared with my husband what was going on with me—for me. My approach was to reveal what I was noticing within myself. I started my story off with, "Here's what was going on in my head . . . "

We get into trouble when we say things to get other people to change, and he could have had a much different reaction. That did not matter to me because my goal was to purge, but in a healthy way. I could feel the toxicity within myself dissipate as I spoke it out loud.

4. **Do a Final Rinse.**

Shift it from present to the past. As I was talking to him, I made sure that I spoke in past tense about the incident, not present. "I felt this way . . . " I thought this way . . . "

This is a neuro-linguistic programming technique that helps your brain to be influenced in subtle ways. It signaled to my brain—and to the hubby—that I had moved beyond any negative feelings. It helped me to release being emotionally charged as if I had already worked through it.

5. **Dry, Fold, and Put Away.**

When you know your laundry is clean, you can shift your attention to drying and folding it, then putting it away. It takes time to dry and finalize the detoxification process. Recovering from the inner critic's attack also takes time.

When you start to fold the laundry, you are purposely transitioning to a state of completion so you can put everything in its proper place. Sometimes it involves you circling back with the other person to close the loop on the conversation before you put it on a shelf. Imagine that you are folding up the inner critic and putting it away.

As I approached this step to work the toxicity out of my head, I was able to fully situate myself as an "observer" of the experience.

The hubby was obviously struggling with his own issues when he got out of bed. Instead of me taking all that on and carrying his emotional load, I reflected back to him. "You seem edgy. What's bothering you and how can I help?" Once I opened up that dialogue, our conversation went to a more productive place where we were honoring each other instead of pummeling one another.

Most people do laundry every week. If you attack the inner critic with the same kind of fervency, you will notice your toxicity getting lighter until it fades.

Activating the 5 steps will be quite a change for you, so start on the *delicate cycle*. I recommend that you bookmark this page or write down the five steps on a card, then keep it close by. When your inner critic shows up, pull out the card and walk through the steps. Even if it feels a little clunky, keep practicing it, so it becomes a normal part of your routine.

I want to share a story that I still have some vulnerability around, but I think it is important for you to understand how this analysis works. I want to preface this with the fact that this is a blast from my past. I want to prepare you to see the birth of an inner critic, in all of its pain and ugliness. My family and I have healed and moved on from our difficult past, but I want to share this story with you so you can learn how discover and shut down inner critics.

STORY: The Birth of an Inner Critic

I was a foster child for a period of time due to some unfortunate life circumstances, and I was quite the rebellious, outspoken gal. My experience in the foster care system was not a good one. Most people meant well, but from the moment I entered into "care" with the foster child label, the difference in treatment was clear. People's perceptions of me were more negative than I was used to. I could read it on their faces, body language, and in their condescending voices. They saw me as damaged and pitiful.

My introspection was confirmed during a difficult time in my life when I had become a chronic runaway. I was 15 and was being held by the sheriff's department after running from my first foster home. It was a nightmare of a place where the foster parents were using the girls as housekeepers, cooks, and yard workers. I remembering feeling exhausted my entire stay.

The foster dad had been eyeballing me in unsavory ways, and it was only a matter of time before I would be in a terrible predicament. I shared my fear with my social worker, but it was clear that I was on my own.

The decision to run was a no-brainer. This was a matter of survival, so I jumped out of a two-story window with a trash bag full of clothes in the middle of the night. I was simply not going to put up with being taken advantage of or being violated against my will.

My 2-day freedom spree ended with a backseat ride to the county jail. My driver was a redheaded and rude sheriff's deputy, *Jim H.* We took an instant disliking to each other. He was a foul-mouthed, heavy-set person who spoke to me with disdain. His tone was condescending and sarcastic, and listening to him lecture me was like listening to a never-ending, high-pitch scream, with a side of nails on a chalkboard. He didn't know me, and he had no idea what was going on in my life, yet he continued to talk to me in a dehumanizing way.

The situation left me vulnerable and frightened. I had resolved in my mind to suck it up and see if I could go home. The relationship with my mom was severely strained, and my dad was caught in the middle of our problems. At least I knew what to expect there, and I could steer clear of any danger. I rationalized that I could deal with it, and I shared my position with the social worker and the sheriff. Here's my recollection of that day:

We walk into a conference room, and my parents are stoic.

We sit, and the social worker starts talking through the events that have taken place. I'm crying quietly.

The social worker finally stops talking, and then turns to me for input. This is hard for me to be vulnerable, but I put it out there.

"I'm ready to come home."

A long pause ensues. I look at them. They aren't looking at me. Mom holds a steely gaze. Dad is shaking and holding back tears. Then he speaks.

"We don't want her back."

BOOM! I am stun-gunned.

Silence lasts forever, and everyone except Mom seems shocked. The trained crisis manager, my social worker, finally speaks.

"Ookkaaayy. Thank you for your time. We will take it from here."

They are talking, but I can't hear them. I can only hear the voice in my head.

You are not wanted. You are not loved. You are being thrown away. No one believes you.

It's my new inner critic being born. I don't know what to call it right now because I am traumatized. I just know it is ugly, and I keep hearing . . .

You are not wanted. You are not loved. You are being thrown away. No one believes you.

Another sheriff's deputy, Brian, reluctantly walks me out of the room. There's no place else for me to go at the moment, so he takes me back to the jailing area. He's a nice guy.

"Don't worry kiddo; I'll go get you a Big Mac. I know you must be starving." *I'm left alone.*

I sob myself to sleep with thoughts of deep rejection, and a personal resolution to never be this vulnerable again. Ever. Ever. Ever!

The Inner Critic Takes Shape

Fast forward to a few months later. I was at a point where I had established a cycle of running away from every foster home I was placed in. I talked to counselors and went through psychological assessments. I was lectured by my social worker and threatened by judges. It just didn't matter to me, and I continued to run because I was angry. Every new foster home served as a reminder that I was not wanted.

I had run so many times that my court status changed from a CHINS (*Child in Need of Services*) to a juvenile delinquent. Here's my recollection of the last runaway experience, which led to that status change:

I'm free once again. I've managed to quietly slip out of the foster home with my trash bag of belongings and meet my friend, Laura. She is waiting down the street in her beat up little car. As I get in, she welcomes me.

"Are you okay?" She is a true friend who has been through a lot. Pregnant and married at 16 to her high school sweetheart, Laura knows my story. I also know she is helping me because she feels guilty.

My mind goes on a side trip, and I recall how Laura's dad frequently took us water skiing on the lake. One afternoon after skiing, we went back to Laura's house. I went down to the basement family room to change and gather my belongings. As I was about to change into my clothes, Laura's dad came down and approached me awkwardly. He had been drinking, and he mumbled some crazy talk. Then he pinched my breast.

I immediately went upstairs and told Laura, who was very embarrassed. This had happened before with someone else. My house was within bike riding distance, so I hopped on my 10-speed and booked it all the way home. When I arrived, I was starting to feel the shock of what happened and felt like I need to do something about it. I grabbed the phone book and found the number of a hotline for teenagers in crisis—I considered a violation of my body a serious crisis.

The lady on the phone wasn't very helpful. She told me to tell my parents, so I reluctantly told my mom, who called Laura's mom, who said, "that's a bunch of crap." Case closed and I was banned from Laura's house forever. I was also labeled a troublemaker.

You are not wanted. You are not loved. You are being thrown away. No one believes you.

But Laura knew the truth about her dad.

I come back from the memory and look at Laura.

"I am better now that I am free." And I sigh with relief.

We immediately head to her trailer, where her husband and small baby are asleep. I crash in the spare bedroom, and for the next two weeks, I feel safe.

The Inner Critic Gets a Name

Two weeks pass. It's a drizzly spring day. Gray day.

The sheriff's car pulls up.

"Go hide in the bathroom!" Laura is frantic but is quickly composing herself.

I curl my 105-pound body into a ball under the bathroom sink hoping to avoid discovery. I listen as they comb the trailer.

The search is over in 5 minutes. The tiny door opens, and I am blinded with flashlights. There stands Deputy Jim H. with his half bald red head. This is the last person I want to see. He grins and laughs. I envision throat-punching him and escaping.

He tells me to get out and slaps handcuffs on me as if I were a serial killer. I hear his annoying grunts like he's at the all-you-can-eat pork barbeque buffet. Is there any way to escape from this devil?

As we walk out to the car, he opens the car door and said something that I will never forget.

"You're nothin' but white trash!"

BOOM! I'm stun-gunned AGAIN. I feel a mental surge of white hot lightning pain go through my body.

You are not wanted. You are not loved. You are being thrown away. No one believes you.

This inner critic now has enough information to officially be named.

It tells me: "White Trash. That's me, and that's you."

It's excruciating to hear. All systems shut down.

Yet, there is a small voice deep inside that tells me I am going to get out of this one day. I don't ever want anyone to feel the way I am feeling in this moment. I am trapped right now, but one day I will help people to overcome this feeling.

And then the *authentic me* goes dormant, taking the remnants of those traumatic days with me for a long time.

Years later, I am reminded of this scene in my life. It's always nipping at my heels and barking in my head. How do I stop it?

I go through the 5-Step Wash Cycle.

1. I allow myself to be with the inner critic that has haunted me. I journal about him, noticing him as I soak in his presence, recognizing when he likes to appear. I notice how he likes to operate, and when he does the most damage to my emotional state.

2. I purposely shift from the negative aspects of the memory to how I have grown as a result of it. I think about why I am thankful for it. I process how it can be useful in my work as an executive coach and consultant. I recognize that I have the power to shut down this inner critic. I accept the power.

3. I begin sharing this story with others, which is painful and leaves me vulnerable. I recognize immediately that I am building resilience to its impact. Each time I share, I gain strength. I notice that others can relate and express their own pain. Sharing is powerful.

4. Every time I share, I intentionally shift from present tense talk to past tense talk. This helps me to put distance between me and the harmful effects of my experience. I refuse to relive the pain because I overcame it a long time ago. I know now that I am

creative, resourceful, and whole. I know that I belong, I am wanted, I am needed, and I am loved.

5. I put the memory to rest. I have come to a place of forgiveness, and I choose not to carry the burden of judgment. God's got my back. I can rest now because I have worked through it.

A Final Word about Inner Critics and Your Inner Committee

I want to come back to your inner committee and tie it all together up to this point. We have committee members who show up as more idealistic and positive, and we have others who are cautious and critical. We need both for good balance in our decision-making. Inner critics try to influence and partner with committee members so they can justify a seat at your table.

For example, let's say you have a committee member called *The Analyst*, who likes to dive into details. *The Analyst* enjoys this and is good at it. Your inner critic, *Perfectionist*, comes along and says, "Now you know you have to analyze every single detail, and you *should* because if you don't get it right, then you will be seen as a liar and people won't trust what you say."

Perfectionist is trying to lay a guilt trip on you and make you responsible for the whole world. So, *Analyst* can entertain this thought and become infected with it. Or, *Analyst* can end this by telling *Perfectionist* to SHUT UP by running Perfectionist through the wash cycle.

The final word (or *words* for those of you who are grammatically correct): You live in choice. Exercise the right to choose who is the boss of you, and who needs to be excused from the committee.

CHAPTER 7

EMOTIONS:
THE PUZZLING PIECE

*"What's emotion got to do with your natural
algorithm? Everything!" -Angie Nuttle*

The next puzzle to solve is to figure out where emotions fit, and they have their place. I've talked to you about pre-existing conditions, written codes, values, inner committees, and inner critics. All of these things feed into your natural algorithm. So, what is the relationship between all of these and your emotions?

Emotions are the glue that binds everything together. They can also jack up everything if you don't manage them effectively.

The fact is that you cannot eliminate emotions out of your life. It is physiologically impossible to shut them down unless you have sustained an injury to a specific part of the brain that governs emotions. For all of you avid researchers, I recommend studying the work of Antonio Damasio, a well-known neuroscientist recognized as the authority on emotions and decision-making.

Damasio has published numerous studies confirming that our decisions are at least 80% emotionally based. When we get up in the morning, we decide what outfit we will wear. We choose what we will eat. We decide if we will be early or late to work. All of these activities require emotion. Even when a person says, "I'm taking the emotion out of this decision," he or she is making an emotional decision.

We are taking time to explore this topic because composing your soul involves governing your emotions, allowing them their place, and quieting them when they want to blow up. These chemically induced responses occur naturally, but we all know they can get out of balance when triggered by external stimuli (stuff happening around you).

All emotions have value.

Some seem more positive and uplifting, like happiness, joy, and surprise; whereas other emotions have a darker side, like sadness, fear, frustration, and anger. Each one allows us to experience something deeper within us for personal growth. It's the dark side of emotions that we have to watch out for, so they don't hang around for an extended period.

The situation to manage is nipping a potential root of bitterness in the bud by identifying emotional triggers. They can be like bombs going off in your head. We need to work on desensitizing them in this next segment.

Understanding Your Emotional Triggers

We all have them. If we don't control them, they can cause us to go from joyful composure to unraveled discombobulation—having a complete meltdown, malfunction, or disorientation. Emotional triggers are embedded into our brains and our hearts because we care about something. I'm not talking about your average level of caring; I'm talking about deep feelings that are tied to personal values and beliefs.

I'm fascinated by people's reactions to political and social issues. We know that today's world is becoming progressively more violent and angry. Emotional triggers are at the heart of this frightening phenomenon. It's clear that something more is going on than just a freedom of expression or a stand for values.

We see more people protesting in the streets. We watch social media being used as a way to yell at our governmental system and to lash out at one another. We witness terrible tragedies where human lives are cut short in large numbers. What we are seeing is a collision between emotional triggers and prolonged stress.

Triggers are most often complicated by daily stressors, which builds up to an emotional eruption. Stress is one of the biggest catalysts of people exploding and losing control of themselves. I don't have to preach to you about what stress does to a person over time. You already know that it erodes your physiological and psychological being.

I equate it to wearing down the brakes in your car. When you constantly ride your brakes, stomp on them, and abuse them over time, they eventually stop working because you've worn away the pads. You begin to hear them scraping against the rotors, and if you keep trying to push through, you find that one day, they give out. Most of us have sense enough to get the car into the shop, but there are those few folks who don't. These are the extremists who inflict damage on the rest of the world.

The best path forward is to do preventive maintenance and change the way you handle the brakes. In other words, you have to proactively deal with your emotional triggers and choose to treat them differently.

STORY: The Head Explosion and What Emotional Triggers Look Like

I believe in treating each person as unique, but equally valuable. One of my emotional triggers centers around my value of respecting others and their uniqueness. I also value protecting the innocent. I want to share a story that reveals how one of my emotional triggers showed up and its impact. Here's my recollection:

It's late in the afternoon.

My daughter, Mackenzie, is playing with her friend "Shauna." These two girls are best buddies and practically inseparable. They love and trust each other.

The doorbell rings.

It's Maddie from down the street. She doesn't like Shauna, which annoys me a little bit. Mackenzie runs downstairs to answer the door, and I see her whispering something back and forth with Maddie, then Maddie leaves.

The next thing I know, I hear Mackenzie talking to Shauna.

"You have to go home now because my mom doesn't want you to be here anymore. "

Did I just hear what I thought I heard? I am stunned. I feel heat rising up my neck as it turns into burning flames upon my cheeks.

Shauna leaves the house quickly as I come around the corner to see what is going on.

Oh no, this will not be happening! I practically run to Mackenzie and confront her as my body trembles with a big adrenaline rush.

Well, that is a bit of an understatement. Let's just say I have a head explosion. An emotional trigger had been hit. I lose it. I yell.

When I think about Mackenzie telling her friend to go home, blaming *me* as the reason, and ultimately fibbing so that she can play with her other friend, it activates a number of value violations for me.

My *Executive Coach* committee member is temporarily disabled. I stop thinking and filtering my words. I forget that I am a corporate talent expert, CEO, and otherwise levelheaded human being. I just react, and the trigger drives me into an angry woman demanding that Mackenzie rectify this situation, *now*.

I march my crying daughter by the arm down to Shauna's house to admit what she has done and apologize to her.

My heart is racing with anger, but also with a compassionate desire to defend Shauna's faithfulness as a good friend. I don't want her to feel like she is less valuable or disposable. I also want her to know that I am not the reason she was told to leave.

Shauna forgives with tremendous ease. I am amazed at her resilience.

Mackenzie is deeply remorseful. She's sobbing, recognizing her mistake. She's learned an important lesson this day, and there's no doubt in my mind that the incident will influence how she shapes her own values.

I finally start to calm down as my body chemicals withdraw from emergency status.

I am happy to say that Mackenzie and Shauna recover from this incident and build back their trust for one another. I also learn some things about myself. I still have a long way to go, even after all these years.

Where Do Triggers Come from?

Triggers don't discriminate between your relationships and your business dealings. They show up whenever they hear their names being called, and if you are also experiencing excessive stress, they can appear in some very unflattering ways.

Where did my response originate? It's the question we should ask ourselves for every trigger that gets in the way of us being productive. I thought about my strong reaction over the next several days, and it came to me.

My mind went back to Mackenzie's little friend. I knew Shauna had been in foster care and was eventually adopted by the people we knew as her parents. That information activated my pre-existing condition around my own foster care experience. I had that filter on, so when I heard Mackenzie telling Shauna to leave, I heard:

You are not wanted. You are not loved. You are being thrown away. No one believes you.

As I watched Shauna leave, I knew that she felt rejected and suddenly not good enough to play at our house. I instantly began duking it out with my inner critic and my pre-existing condition. My values were being stepped on, which kicked my tail into gear to stand up for her. She felt like trash being thrown away, and I needed her to know that I would not ever let that happen.

To sum it up, emotional triggers can be activated by sensitivity around:

- Inner critics
- Pre-existing conditions
- Values that are getting stepped on

The desensitization process takes great self-awareness and pre-planning. The purpose of what we are about to do is designed to disrupt a pattern. We aren't going to erase your emotions and turn you into a robot. We are simply going to take the raw emotions you feel, associate them with the root cause, and funnel the energy into a more productive process.

Exercise: How to Desensitize Your Emotional Triggers

There are two parts to the exercise. First, we will do some trigger identification and reflection. Second, we will create an *Emotional Trigger Action Plan*. We will call this the ETAP for brevity's sake.

1. **Trigger Identification:** This is an exercise I normally do in coaching engagements. I recommend you talk this through with someone you trust. In your journal, jot down your answers to the following questions:

   - Think about a time when you totally lost your cool. Describe what happened. Be sure to capture what feelings showed up for you.
   - Which of your values were stepped on?
   - Was there a pre-existing situation that played into your reaction?
   - Was an inner critic present? Who was it and what did he/she say?

Take a couple of days to reflect on your responses. Go back to that day when you lost your cool. Is there anything new that you notice about it? About yourself? Is there anything that is unresolved? What is it you need to overcome? You don't have to have a solution yet, just allow yourself to process this trigger and its origin thoroughly.

2. **Create your ETAP**: It's time to purposely change the way you view everything. Instead of thinking about how upset you were that day, think about what you want to change about your reaction. You have to a) picture what a different reaction looks like; and b) create a canned response for the future.

- Imagine you can go back in time to that memory and alter your reaction. In your journal, write down what the new reaction would look like.
- How would your expression appear? How would you carry your body?
- Change the words you spoke at that time to a more calm, thought-out statement. Write it down in your journal.
- Is there a curious question you could have asked rather than making a judging statement? If so, what could it have been? Write it down.
- How would you like the new reaction to end? (Throat punching is not an option.)

Once you rewrite your story, play it out in your head and see yourself in the calm state. You will then want to create a personal script to manage this trigger and practice speaking it out loud. We tend to act upon our triggers when we don't know what to say. Provide yourself with the words that need to be said to yourself, and also to the other person. For example, if you know you have a trigger around feeling excluded, you might create a mental script for yourself like this:

Mental Script: *I notice that I am feeling excluded. There's an inner critic who wants to harass me and egg me on.*

I am choosing to be on the outside of it and see it for what it is. I may process this later with a friend or in my journal, but right now, I am here to notice.

Let's say that another person is involved whom you view as the button pusher. You might create a script like this:

Button Pusher Script: *I notice that when you are talking to everyone else at the party, you and I aren't communicating much. What's your observation? Let's talk about it.*

You will want to funnel your energy to a controlled conversation. If you struggle with this, you will want to learn how to create something I call an *auto responder*. We will discuss that in one of the upcoming chapters.

Practicing the scripts will help you develop control and self-discipline around your emotions. You want to talk about something calmly, and if you just can't do it, use the script, but continue to go back and work through steps 1 and 2.

There's always a story here from people, and it starts with *but.*

But that person is a bully. I can't talk to him!"

But she was insulting my child. I had to cuss her out, or my kid would think I was weak!"

But he just bulldozed over me, and I had put up with it long enough!"

Right now, I want to encourage you to stay the course, continue the work on yourself, and then we will deal with the *buts* later in the book.

Up to this point, we've gone through a number of elements that relate to your overall Natural Algorithm. Let's bring it all together in the next chapter by creating your operational story.

CHAPTER 8

CAPTURE YOUR NATURAL ALGORITHM STORY

"You aren't supposed to fit. You are here for a mission!" -Angie Nuttle

All of us have felt a sense of pressure to be like others, to fit in, to cut parts of ourselves out of a situation, to act and behave like everyone else. The corporate world has long been known for trying to create employees who look, think, and act alike. Leadership programs and training trying to produce cookie-cutter leaders, and when someone doesn't fit their model, he or she is politely shoved out.

Have you ever felt like this was happening to you?

You may sense that it is going on now at work or in a certain organized body that you belong to. You don't quite fit, or something doesn't align. You come home from work feeling exhausted, and you barely get supper made before you plop down on the couch with a bottle of wine or a bag of greasy potato chips. That exhaustion is coming from the prolonged denial of who you genuinely are as a human being.

You may be showing up with parts of yourself, but not fully. Can you imagine not having your arms, a leg, and an ear? That's what you are essentially doing when you aren't able to bring forth the fullness of who you are.

I know this sounds fatalistic, but when you are in an environment that doesn't support most of your natural algorithm, it tells me that you are using an inordinate amount of energy to live in a world that is contrary to you being you. It becomes toxic to all parties involved.

You are not here to be a clone.

On the flip side of that, recognize that everyone around you has a different algorithm, so there has to be an appreciation of that fact. You may need to make some small concessions. However, if you find you are sacrificing most of your values and beliefs, then the money, time, and effort you are putting in are absolutely not worth it.

This is your wake-up call. Do you hear it?

I'm telling you, you are not designed to look or even act like everyone else.

You may like the feeling of being molded and shaped by other people, but if you want to compose your soul, that molding and shaping need to complement the natural flow of who you are so you can live with your daily decisions in life.

Freedom, independence, and a sense of peace are contrary to living in corporate business prison. Defeat the cloning processes that are being imposed upon you and start to create your own mold. I'm not telling you to leave your current job (unless you absolutely want to), but I am telling you to live true to your natural algorithm, which includes your values.

Am I telling you to rebel? Heck yes!

People are waiting for you to show up and inspire them with your gifts. That crazy idea you thought of, but you poo-pooed before it had a chance to germinate? Revive it! That voice that tells you to stand up against that coworker in the meeting who treats everyone like idiots? Listen to it and act! That idea to start a new business? Jump off the cliff and do it!

Come back to you, and meet the real you. #ubu (you be you).

STORY: Snapshot of an Operational Story and Natural Algorithm

We are about to embark on a couple of exercises that will help you on the path of rediscovery. I will take you through a series of questions, then challenge you to write your operational story. An operational story articulates how you like to function in the world, the way you like to *show up on a daily basis*. I am providing a personal example of what one might look like:

I am multi-faceted and an achieving activator. There are circumstances in which I thrive that most people balk at. It's normal for me to have several major things going on at one time, and I like it. For example, at the writing of this book, I am in the process of selling a house, building a new one, running a business, onboarding new clients, and chauffeuring my mom and daughter around to the places they need to be. Most writers would gasp at this.

"How can you even think?" The typical writer has to go away, be inspired by ocean waves or nature to process a book. Not me. I am writing it in chunks in between being a working business owner and parent who helps her kid with homework, getting ready for school, and cheerleading competitions.

Humans are creatures of habit. I am no different.

As a consultant, I go through an interesting cycle as I prepare for an event.

I'm excited by possibility, which is a prominent value for me. Once the possibility becomes a reality, I go into full strategic planning mode. I figure out how much time I have until I need to have materials ready, communications, and keynote speaking topics. I map it out on a calendar to hold the time and space for the work. I typically like to get it all done just inside of a deadline.

I find myself always trying to maximize the time and use every minute. I typically reprioritize but know whatever I push back, I will get done later. I build up like a pressure cooker in the time leading up to the event; I give every inch of my focus during the event, and then after the event, I go into an "I am not doing ANYTHING for the next 24 hours" mode. It's like my reward. I have given everything, and I have used all reserves, now I can rest peacefully.

Keynotes are a different animal for me. It takes me longer to figure out what I am going to talk about, so I will allow a time of just brainstorming and capturing random thoughts over a period of time. Almost every time, I figure it out right before I am about to speak. There is something about it that is more authentic and spontaneous, which fulfills me, and aligns with my values.

I know that in the few days before, an inner critic is going to pop up to interfere with my focus, so I will go to battle with it by getting into my morning devotion time, capturing some key scriptures to combat it and battling the inner critic with those scriptures. It works every time. I trust that everything that will come out of my mouth will be inspired by a deeper belief and faith.

I notice that a transition occurs when I return from a successful event and keynote. I enjoy operating in my mission, and because I put everything into it, I usually come home completely tapped out.

Another value kicks in—cleanliness. I struggle with this one because I have a pre-existing condition that I can't sit down and relax if everything is strewn about the house. It just so happens that my husband and daughter don't have cleanliness as their top priority, so we clash. Some of you ladies can understand where I am coming from.

It can become a source of irritation after I have been standing on my feet all day exerting constant focus, to come home to a messy house. I have to use self-talk to get through my flaring hot attitude.

- *They've just been trying to survive while I was gone.*
- *They spent more time focusing on fun instead of picking up things.*
- *They didn't do this intentionally to upset me.*

The truth is that they have a different algorithm than I do. They value different things, and they value spending their time differently. They don't have a hang-up of order and cleanliness like I do. They can sit in a pile of socks, pizza boxes, and strewn clothing like it's a luxury swimming pool. They are happy and having fun.

What do I do? I move along my algorithm; I pick up a few things because it makes me more comfortable and aligned with what I value. Then I sit down and enjoy the evening. I may even go to bed early to completely wind down. I am a researcher, and many nights I get inspired around 10:30 p.m., and end up creating something new to explore the next day.

From a daily life perspective, I find ways to laugh every day because it is another source of fuel for me. I also do other things to take care of myself, like managing my daily diet, walking, and talking with my family.

I must have coffee before talking to anyone, so I don't schedule appointments before 9 a.m. My conceptual and idea brain is wide awake in the mornings, then after lunch, my mind tends to focus on more tactical, analytical tasks. Toward the end of the day, I scurry to score completion points with myself by doing final sweeps of my email, making my priority list for the next day, then walking out of my office no later than 5:30 p.m. My least optimal and most irritable time during the day is usually between 4 and 6 p.m.

I need the freedom to be spontaneous, creative, and strategic. I don't like boundaries and parameters, and that is why I am an entrepreneur. I can sometimes be fatalistic and a perfectionist, but I am resilient. I value respect. If I feel disrespected, it impacts my energy and effort. I overcome mistakes easily and move on to be even more inspired.

I fight for people, and I am driven to encourage them. I break them out of prison and help them find freedom. My mantra or constant theme is Isaiah 61. It is my mission. This is why I am here at this time in this world:

"The Spirit of the Lord God is upon me; because the Lord has anointed me to preach good tidings unto the meek; He has sent me to bind up the brokenhearted, to proclaim freedom to the captives, and the opening of the prison to them that are bound." Isaiah 61:1 (King James Version)

In simplified language, I get people out of their personal prisons. I encourage them, challenge them, and guide them. I help them to be seen, heard, valued, and celebrated. The entire chapter is relevant in my life, but these first two verses sum up my life's mission.

Create Your (Operational) Natural Algorithm Story

What is your natural state of being? There are so many idiosyncrasies in how you operate. Begin to create the story of who you are. Your assignment now is to gather as much information about yourself over the next 13 weeks.

I recommend that you do a daily journal check-in where you write down a realization about the way you operate each day. If you don't recognize anything new, no problem. Move on to the next day.

I also want you to process as many of your realizations as possible, so I have created a list of questions for you to work through in the next exercise. This is a big list that will take time. If it's part of your algorithm to plow through it, then go ahead. If you want to take your time, pace yourself.

Exercise: Begin to Capture Your Natural Algorithm

This is a great exercise to talk through with someone to gain insight on how you like to operate. Be sure to capture the highlights in your journal. To get deeper reflection, I have broken it up into weeks for those who need established timelines to follow.

Week 1: Warm-up Questions:
- What are the first 5 words that come to mind when you think about who you are?
- What words do not describe you?
- What action words fit your style (i.e., driver, achiever, cat herder)?
- How do other people describe you (both positive and critical feedback)?
- What do you do to have fun?

- What books do you read?
- In general, how do you like to operate?

Week 2: Daily Energy Peaks and Valleys:
- What points of the day do you have your most energy?
- What points of the day do you have the least amount of energy?
- When is your best time for thinking conceptually about ideas and possibilities?
- When is your best time for thinking about numbers, analytics, and details?
- When is your most productive time of the day when you get the most done?
- How would you describe your rest cycle, or the times when you absolutely have to rest?

Week 3: Routines and Schedules:
- What do you generally do in your first hour of the day?
- What do you generally do at the end of your day?
- What is your eating routine?
- What is your exercise routine (if you have one)?
- What is your sleeping routine?
- What are some of your regularly scheduled events or activities?
- What other routines do you have that haven't been mentioned?

Week 4: Your Physical Space
- What is your ideal physical space?

- Do you lean more towards hoarding and clutter, or minimalism and order?
- Do you like colorful or neutral surroundings?
- What makes you very comfortable in your space?
- What makes you very uncomfortable in your space?
- What's your position on proximity (do you like things or people close or far away)?
- Do you prefer apartments, subdivisions, or farms?

Week 5: Your Relationships

- What is the ideal relationship to you?
- How important are relationships to you in general?
- Do you have lots of friends, or a few (or just one)?
- What is the state of your relationship with your family?
- What is the state of your relationship with your friends?
- How would you describe your approach to relationships?
- How do you handle disagreements?
- How do you express your love?
- What's your view on sexual relationships?
- Would you describe yourself as highly sexual, average, or non-sexual?

Week 6: Your Work

- What type of work do you do?
- Do you like what you are doing now?
- What's the ideal work situation for you?
- At work, do you focus more on performance or people?
- What do you avoid at work?
- What do you gravitate toward at work?
- When do you feel successful?
- When do you feel you've failed?
- What is your work style?
- What do you dislike about work?

Week 7: Your Downtime

- Do you take downtime? Why or why not?
- When do you believe it's okay to slow down?
- Do you like to slow down? If so, when?
- Do you prefer beaches, mountains, or amusement parks?
- Which do you like better, alone time or being around others in your downtime?
- How much downtime is enough?
- What happens when you don't get it?

Week 8: Your Habits

- What personal habits do you have?
- What behavioral habits do you have?
- What do your driving habits look like?
- What habits serve you the best?
- When do your habits get you in trouble?

Week 9: Your Sayings and Mantras

- What sayings do you use frequently?
- What are your favorite lines, verses, or quotes?
- What is your mantra?
- What words do you use consistently?

Week 10: Mental Health Questions

- What do you avoid?
- What do you gravitate toward?
- When are the times when you function at your best?
- When are the times you function at your worst?
- When do you believe it's okay to hurry up?
- Do you like to hurry? If so, when?
- How do you respond to and manage crises?
- What bores you?
- Do you prefer to listen, see, or act first?

Week 11: Physical Health Questions

- How do you describe your physical health?
- What level of physical activity do you practice?
- What level of physical activity do you prefer?
- Do you go to doctors and dentists?
- What's your position on traditional versus alternative medicine?
- When do you typically get sick?
- When is your physical health usually at its best?

Week 12: Emotional Health Questions

- In what ways do you feel successful in life?
- How do you like to celebrate success?
- How do you handle failure and mistakes?
- What makes you laugh?

- What is your approach to highly emotional situations?
- Which words in the following list describe you best from an emotional standpoint?

  - Even keeled
  - Detached
  - Overly Emotional
  - Frustrated
  - Stressed
  - Depressed
  - Angry
  - Joyful
  - Content
  - Complacent
  - On auto-pilot
  - Bipolar
  - Insecure
  - Reactive
  - Calm
  - Other words that fit your emotional state

Week 13: Spiritual Health Questions

- Do you see yourself as spiritual?
- How do you demonstrate your spirituality?
- If you aren't spiritual, how do you view others who are?
- Do you believe there is a higher power?
- What spiritual activities or rituals do you participate in?
- Do you have a particular faith? If so what is it?
- What does spirituality give you?
- If you are not spiritual, what prevents you from it?

Once you ponder these questions and go over the highlights in your journal, put them away for a week. Plan a time to be alone and review what you wrote. Take a highlighter and mark the keywords or phrases that resonate with you the most. Your goal here is to begin distilling down what you've identified in your reflections.

I recommend that you create a short story about yourself that captures the essence of you. The highlighted data can be used in your story. The purpose of the story is to see who you are at your core and even create a new title for yourself. All of this will help you to gain clarity on what your mission is, and what it is that you are being called to do before you leave this life.

CHAPTER 9

EMOTIONAL COMPOSURE 101

"Achieving composure is like being in the eye of the hurricane. You simply have to shift with the center, or you'll find yourself in the damaging winds."
-Angie Nuttle

You want the events of your life to go smoothly. You envision peace. You see yourself doing what you love without opposition. You imagine the celebration of your success, and it feels great. For this to become a reality, the flow of your day has to work just right, so all of these pieces fit together. This is you being a composed soul.

When you are flowing according to your natural algorithm, everything is fantastic, and a sense of calm is present. Emotions, however, can cause static in your mind so that you aren't getting the proper *orders of operation* through to your brain. Emotions can be disruptive to your thinking process and cause you to be less effective in your daily operations. Life becomes more complicated when you bring other people into the picture who have:

- A different algorithm

- Lowered levels of self-awareness and emotional intelligence
- A bully or bulldozer mentality

You can have a process that you like to follow, but if people are not respectful of it, it will pose a number of challenges for you that will require emotional composure. I was reminded of this as I was taking my daughter to school on my way to work.

STORY: The Car-Rider Lines

My daughter was a bus rider all of her young life until we started building a new house. Our primary home sold faster than we anticipated, so we moved in temporarily with my mother. I had to change my schedule to drive her to school, and that's how I became a car-rider parent.

Every parent who has a car-rider knows that you have to fight the car-rider lines. If you don't arrive early, you will face long lines waiting for the drop off point. Arriving just in time or afterward will slow you down.

I've also learned that there are certain respect and courtesy norms that car-rider parents practice. For example, traffic is coming from both ways when entering the parking lot line where parents drop off their children at the door. There is an unspoken understanding that drivers allow each other to take turns to file into the single lane of traffic to the school door. It's the polite thing to do.

This unspoken understanding works well and keeps the traffic moving in an even flow. Occasionally, a car-rider parent will violate this norm. The parent is so anxious to get ahead that he/she breaks the order, cutting in front of another parent. This leaves the offending parent in the middle of the road, blocking traffic, and causing tempers to flare because the unspoken rule has been broken.

It's a testament to the violating parent's lack of self-awareness, and how it impacts other parents. Not only is that parent unaware of his or her impact, but it appears to other parents that that person has a lack of consideration and respect for other people. To make matters worse, the violating parent tends to always look straight ahead, pretending the other car-riders don't exist.

When people feel that they are being "run over" and ignored, this causes an activation of emotional triggers. The "victims" are left to fume over the violation, and herein lies the potential for emotional composure to disappear. Here's my recollection of one of those mornings:

On this particular morning, the emotional reactions are palpable.

Mackenzie and I are in the car watching the violation happening in real time. A parent has cut in line at the turn and has blatantly ignored the unspoken rules. This parent seems to lack emotional intelligence.

Even though all parents are in their cars, the tension is felt in the air and directed at the violating parent. Disapproving looks and flying hands in the air express their sentiments. Yes, getting out of order and causing a disruption to the flow signals a flagrant disregard for the car-rider norm.

Thoughts are running through my head. I am gritting my teeth.

What are you doing, lady? This is so rude!

My emotional composure is starting to deteriorate. My inner committee member, *Executive Coach*, is desperately trying to coach me to be cool.

As a result of the violator lady's disrespect, it takes much longer to get to through the line for all of the parents. Traffic is backed up all the way down a major road. Buses can't get into the school parking lot, and I am sure many people are frustrated because they are now going to be late to work.

Ironically, the violator lady doesn't get out of the line any faster, although I'm sure her goal was to get ahead faster, be first, and get out of there. She jacked it all up for herself.

This incident has other effects.

When I finally get close to the door, I am third in line when we come to a stop. Usually, at this point, it's safe for the kids to go ahead and jump out of the car and go into the school. I am staring at my daughter and zoning out because I am thinking about the violation of that offending parent and how I would love to karate chop that smirk off her face. Right when I see it happening in my mind . . .

"Mom!"

Mackenzie is sitting there staring back at me.

Two cars move up, and I have to move up in line. I ask Mackenzie why she didn't get out at the drop off point.

She laughs at me and says, "Mom, I was looking at you to unlock the door because I couldn't get out!"

I chuckle. Wow, I must really be losing it. (My emotional composure, that is!)

I totally missed her signal because I was distracted by the norm violation and how I felt like throat-punching that person (which is completely contrary to a composed response).

I hug her as she gets out of the car and goes into the school. Then I go about my way.

It leaves me thinking, "Why do people need to be first? What drives us to behave in such a ridiculous way that we bulldoze over people, pretend they aren't there and get stuck in our own mistakes? How am I being affected by the *Need To Be First Syndrome?*"

A more important question is, "How do I become more emotionally composed?"

Emotional Intelligence and Composure: Know the Rules and Keep Your Cool

Emotional intelligence and emotional composure are partners. The first one requires knowledge. The second one requires a special kind of mental toughness. They both require three things:

- Self-awareness
- Managing your emotions
- Wearing other's' shoes (not literally, but figuratively speaking)

If you think about the car-rider process to get to the school, it's similar to emotional intelligence at work and is knowledge-based. You may have written rules, but most of the cultural rules are unwritten. People are expected to *know* the rules, abide by them, and respect each other.

It's easy to see the car-rider violation as disrespectful and lacking emotional intelligence, but what about the people who are impacted? From a composure standpoint, they are challenged as well. Not only do they have to practice emotional intelligence, but they have to practice composure. Otherwise, they are just as guilty as the car-rider lady. They are *us*. You and me.

A person who practices high emotional composure is going to have an empathetic and curious view of the people around them. They recognize that they have an impact on people, and if they don't compose themselves, it ends up impacting not just one person but an entire organization (or everyone in the car-rider line!).

But, What If You've Been Blindsided?

What if you are minding your own business and someone blatantly and suddenly wreaks havoc on your world? It happens to the best of us, even me, Angie Nuttle, the person writing from an expert's perspective.

I want to take a moment to point this out: Most people's reactions to a blindside or unexpected behavior are dependent upon the relationship with the attacker. I can split it into two main categories: business and personal.

People are less likely to react strongly in the moment when blindsided in a business situation. It doesn't mean they aren't impacted by what is happening; it just means they are applying the "socially acceptable behavior" filter. Their reactions will come out in other ways, like discussing what happened with a coworker or with a group in the meeting after the meeting. Organizations are notorious for being the big house of passive-aggressive people. You may not know exactly where people stand on a topic, but people are masters at indirectly sharing their feelings.

Bullies are the exception to the rule and are more likely to react aggressively in the moment. This can be attributed to their lack of self-awareness, thoughtlessness of other people, and their need to win. The bully has an "I'm okay, but you are not" mentality, which is deeply rooted in insecurity and fear. Even so, most still have a "socially acceptable behavior" filter if the person blindsiding them is someone in authority over them. Then they can really turn on the charm.

There's also a small population of a few brilliant people who work through their emotional triggers quickly. They get into an "Adult role" and focus on the solution versus the person who is showing up as a rebellious child. Everyone typically likes and appreciates the balance of the adult person.

The calm one. The composed one. The solid rock.

Composure goes much deeper than just putting on a happy or stoic face when norms are violated. If you are composed, you have a strong, resilient center, like the eye of the hurricane, where you are not moved by the gale force winds and debris flying in the air. You remain constant when everything else is swirling around you.

An Example of Business Versus Personal Reactivity

We are apt to have stronger reactions to our personal situations because we have complicated emotional ties to the people we are dealing with. For example, if you find out that your spouse misappropriates funds in your bank account, and you discover this one day as you are looking at your balance, you are likely to confront your spouse with heated anger.

"What the heck is going on? You took $4,600 out of the account and spent it, even though we agreed to use our finances another way? I'm ready to throat-punch you right now!"

You may choose to sulk, be angry, and call your best friend to complain about the stupid move your spouse made. And what really aggravates you is that you won't get a vacation this year.

Change the scenery to a business setting. Your leader decides to take $4,600 out of your departmental budget without discussing it with you. You find out later as you are reviewing your budget that the money was used to cover an executive team-building event where they created haiku poems. What would your reaction be? Maybe a little disgusted and sarcastic, but not as angry because that's your leader, and she is the boss. You might sound something like this:

"Well, I realized my budget was missing, and I didn't even know. I know Haiku poems are important, but I am disappointed because I had plans for that budget money. Oh well."

Do you see the difference between business versus personal reactivity?

I can say with confidence that a blindside response is also dependent on:

- The frequency of occurrences
- Pre-existing conditions
- Your written code

If something happens for the first time and it's completely unexpected, you really do have a genuine shock experience. For example, you are at work sitting in your team meeting. Your leader stands up and announces there's a reduction in force and your department is being eliminated.

Surprise!

What if, on the other hand, your leader is known for having an annual reduction in force and makes this announcement for the fourth year in a row? You are going have a completely different emotional response, like worry or anxiety, but not an electrical jolt running through your body.

Think about your written code and how you are wired to take in information and process it. What if your default response is to internalize bad news and shut down emotionally until you can examine the data? Or you have a pre-existing condition where you had an abusive father, and you learned:

"If I am just quiet, I won't get my head knocked off, and this will all just go away."

I am saying all this to point out that you are normal and so are most of the people around you. So let's figure out how to grow-up in our minds and behave like the big and smart people we are longing to be.

TOOL: Get over a Blindside (or any other situation that awakens your triggers) with E.S.P.

Responding to a blindside and rebounding from it is complex and takes disciplined practice. Composing your emotions intelligently is the key to successfully navigating through the situation. This means showing up in the Adult role as opposed to Child or Parent role.

How do you know if you are in one of these roles? Some of the basic characteristics of people operating in *Child* role include:

- Pouts or sulks
- Complains and blames
- Gossips/talks behind someone's back/passive aggressive
- Throws a fit
- Rebels "I'm not doing that!" (or cuts in line)
- Withdraws

Being in the *Parent* role looks like this:

- Talks down to someone
- Berates others
- Lectures

- Shows up as condescending
- Micromanages
- Uses threatening language or gestures

The *Adult* role looks like this:

- Actively Listens
- Asks curious questions
- Demonstrates compassion and empathy
- Focuses on the situation instead of the person
- Recognizes own mistakes and admits them
- Calms the situation

The skill to be mastered is practicing composure through a tool I have created called E.S.P.:

E- Emotion
S- Switch
P- Presence

E.S.P. is very effective for changing your internal processing experience in the moment. It's also a great way to reconfigure your written code. Here's how it works:

1. **EMOTION:** When you experience a stimulus (i.e. someone blindsides you, or you are exposed to a surprising event that evokes a negative feeling), recognize and name the specific feeling you are having at that very moment. It could be anger, frustration, anxiety, fear, sadness, embarrassment, or something else. Picture that emotion spelled out in your mind. See each letter, each word in bold. Seeing it in your mind helps you to recognize it is there, and also redirects

your emotional energy into a productive thought process.

2. **SWITCH**: Identify the role you are playing in: child, parent, or adult. It's rare that our initial response is in the Adult role unless you've already trained yourself to respond with a tool like E.S.P. You are likely showing up in Parent or Child role. It is what it is, so own your role. Now, intentionally tell your mind to SWITCH to the Adult role, like this:

    "I'm in Child role, and I will now SWITCH to the Adult role. I am choosing to operate in the Adult role now."

    I know this seems weird, but it works when you practice it regularly. You are giving your mind a communication construct, you are telling it what to do, and you are in control of it. You are also disrupting the energy flow that is funneling into whatever negative emotion you are experiencing.

3. **PRESENCE:** It's time to envision yourself as showing up with a peaceful presence, and stepping right into it. I normally encourage people to see themselves being calm. I also have them notice how still they can be. For some, they need to visualize something else, like a forest or a body of water. For example:

Imagine that you are standing at the edge of a pond. A rock has been thrown in it, and you have the ability to slow down the ripples. Watch the ripples flatten out by using your mind to tell it to be still. Think this until the water eventually stops moving. Draw that calm energy into your body, mind, and soul, like it's a soothing salve washing over you.

The first few times you practice the tool, it involves a conscious effort to pull yourself away from the magnetism of your feelings. Weird, but true; we are fascinated with feelings, especially anger. Have you ever been angry and just bathed in it? There's some semblance of power or energy in it that is oddly attractive, so we tend to hang out there longer than necessary.

So, if someone has wronged us and then admits it, we might say, "Okay, I forgive you." But then, we might hold onto the anger for a little while because we like the power, and we like to know that we are justified in some way. It eventually dissipates as new experiences happen and life goes on.

You may be thinking, "Wow, do I have time to do all this E.S.P. stuff when I have been blindsided?" The answer is yes. Your mind can process these three steps very quickly. Over time, it will become a part of your written code and will be much more natural to you. You can also buy more time for internal processing with an auto responder statement, like:

- "That's interesting. Tell me more about that."
- "Thanks for letting me know. I was unaware that was happening. Tell me more."
- "You are clearly bothered by this. I'd like to learn more about what you're thinking."

E.S.P. is also a great *in-the-moment* tool for those persistent and toxic thoughts that keep coming back after you've worked to defuse them.

Let's say that you are struggling with a colleague who continually disrespects you. He frequently barges into your office when you are on client calls, he interrupts and talks over you when you are speaking, and he breaks his verbal commitments he's made to you on a regular basis.

E.S.P. won't solve the bigger underlying issue, but it will help get you in a place where you can think more clearly about the situation without hiring a hit man.

If you want to solve your problems and challenges effectively, you need to be in the Adult role. If you aren't, then the Child role will probably have you crying to every person who will listen. After a while, people get tired of hearing the blamer and complainer because they have their own problems. They don't want to listen to more blaming and complaining, and you become an energy suck. The Parent role will have you micromanaging and bullying everyone while you kill their joy with lecturing and threats.

People will then start avoiding you.

Your 3 Choices

Getting your emotions under control through E.S.P. will help you to take the next step: Processing what you've experienced and coming to a decision about the actions you will take. This is where you are able to make progress as you process your choices in any given scenario. Here are the three main choices you have:

1. You can change the way you are seeing or reacting to the situation, then take action.
2. You can do nothing, and it will stay the same.
3. You can leave, quit, or stop.

Think about your life. If you could apply a percentage of time to each of these choices to indicate how often you practice each one, what would it look like? Would you say that 50% of the time, you do nothing? How about the percentage of time you actually change your perception or reaction? How often do you just quit or walk away? These are great questions to ponder because your choices result in the current outcomes you are getting.

I want to be clear that there is a time and season for each kind of choice. Unfortunately, most people hover around choice #2 and do nothing. Being in a state of choice is incredibly powerful, and you have the power to change everything about your life.

If you have a desire to compose your soul, recognize this important truth: You live in choice every moment. When you don't make a choice, you are still choosing. Where in your life are you choosing to do nothing?

Let's revisit our colleague who keeps barging in and breaking all of the socially acceptable rules known to humankind. You've learned to get your emotions in check through E.S.P., and now you need to deal with a more pervasive problem, the other person. Remember you have three basic choices, and chances are that choice #2 hasn't been working for you. Doing nothing is not an option.

Here's where I wish I could give you the magic problem-solver wand so you can wave it over other people and make them change their ways. Your first step is to realize you simply are not going to change other people. Can you influence them? Yes, but you cannot change them. That is a choice they have to make for themselves. I talk more about how to deal with difficult people in an upcoming chapter about bullies.

Everyone comes with their own set of pre-existing conditions, written code, and natural algorithms. No two people are exactly alike, although they may have some crossover in the way they operate.

What is the best course of action when it comes to other people? Manage yourself and, with a curious approach, meet them where they are at.

CHAPTER 10

BEFORE YOU RULE OTHERS, RULE YOURSELF

"Discipline is the most powerful form of freedom one can experience." -Angie Nuttle

Do you have rule over yourself? When something happens to awaken your emotions, are you able to guide them into submission? Or do they dictate what you do?

You give your power away whenever you choose to let bullies and other strong-willed people pull at your emotions. When you listen to inner critics and pre-existing conditions, they will have you believe that someone else's behavior is caused by you, or you are responsible for their actions. This is a big fat lie.

I struggle with this from time to time, just like you. If I am running a program and someone wants to drop out, *Perfectionist* shows up and blames me.

"If you would have just done_____better, this person would have stayed in the program. You weren't perfect. Something is wrong with you."

I've learned that people's choices don't necessarily have to do with me. What I find is that their choices are based on their own internal and life struggles.

I recently had a wonderful lady drop out of her coaching program because she had too many things on her plate. When I dug deeper, it turns out that she was feeling guilty that she was spending money on herself, and her Should-itis inner critic (otherwise known as *Should-Ann)* was telling her she should be bringing in more money instead of spending it. In this case, she let her *Should-Ann* win.

If you don't want others to rule you, then you will want to turn up your self-awareness. If you tune in closely, you can catch the manifestation of your emotions before they surprise you. Pre-existing conditions and inner critics create invisible prisons that can keep you trapped in your current circumstances. It's worthwhile to understand these internal influencers because they embed emotions inside you that you may not be conscious of.

Just like the wonderful lady I mentioned, you can get way off course in terms of your mission because your vision is clouded. The result can be that you end up mistakenly honoring one thing over something else, and your values become misaligned.

Your fiercest battle is within yourself.

Let's consider dieting as an example. People fail because they don't have rule over their spirit. I can create a future state goal of losing 15 lbs., but that isn't going to get me there. It takes a mindset, determination, and a discipline that just doesn't happen haphazardly or by thinking, "Maybe I can do this today." Instead, you have to think, "I WILL do this, and I AM doing this." I have to decide:

1. What is the goal and why is it important to my value system?
2. What are the obstacles (including inner critics) and how will the goal take priority?
3. What is the tactical plan to go to war with each of those obstacles?
4. How and when do I put the goal in play using small chunks or pieces?
5. I *will* get back up immediately when a setback happens.

Being realistic is important. You will have setbacks, but you have to envision yourself getting back up after a fall. Every situation is an entity unto itself. In dieting, every meal is an entity unto itself. Many of us think if we splurge at dinner, it's all over and we might as well eat everything in sight. It's a fatalistic stance that has to be shut down, both in your dieting *and* your life circumstances.

There's a more effective mindset that has to kick in, which includes:

- Trusting that you can accomplish the goal in front of you
- Committing your way to this path
- Delighting in what you are doing and who you are becoming
- Resting in the plan

Speak life into this plan and mute any voices of fatalism. You've been shutting down your values long enough. Fight to honor them no matter what inner critic or emotion is trying to run interference. I'm not just talking about staying on your diet; I'm talking about every goal you establish for yourself.

Exercise: Examine Your Goals and Mindset

Think of a recent goal you had and analyze it with the following questions:

1. What was the goal and why was it important to your value system?
2. What obstacles did you need to be aware of?
3. Did you have a plan to deal with them? If not, what happened?
4. What were the successful outcomes?
5. What didn't work out, and how did you handle it?

Run this goal through the mindset filters and reflect on each one:

- Trusting that you can accomplish this goal
- Committing your way to this path
- Delighting in what you are doing and who you are becoming
- Resting in the plan

Which ones were easy?
Which ones did you have trouble with?
Explore this in your journal.

STORY: From Calamity and Chaos to Composure

The weekend had been stressful. We had to move out of our old house since the new owners would be moving in soon. I was slightly annoyed because the hubby didn't realize the magnitude of everything we had to do. He approved a birthday party sleepover for my daughter and five friends as if it was a simple feat to take in stride. Here's my recollection of the events that followed:

I'm recoiling inside. Every breath is exhausting this morning. After seeing each little girl leave, disheveled hair from the sleepless night of girliness, it's time to turn our attention to getting all the boxes out of here on our last day on Woodfield Drive.

The day is long, but we manage to survive it and get everything moved. We are facing one last hurdle: The king size mattress we have slept on for ten years. It's like handling a jellyfish down the curvy staircase, and we awkwardly get it out to the truck. I think I have torn my rotator cuff, but I can't worry about that now. We have to change our plan of giving the mattress to my sister after we get a look at the mattress in broad daylight.

It is surely a biohazard. A few months earlier, Aaron sustained a head injury, and it bled into the mattress unbeknownst to me. Oh yeah, is that a dog pee stain in the middle? This big absorbent mattress is a goner. At this point, we decide we have to take it to the dumpster at Aaron's work. We load it in the truck.

We realize we are starving. We also have to pick up Kenzie from cheerleading practice, so we go through the Kentucky Fried Chicken, which is nearby. We notice that the mattress is starting to unfold, so Aaron jumps in back trying to get it situated. I decide to take pictures because we are both laughing so hard at what this must look like: two people dressed like hobos getting a big bloody mattress under control at the KFC. Appetizing, right?

Later, we arrive at my mom's house because she's invited us to stay there while we are building our house. She's out of town, so we let ourselves in.

"It's freezing in here! What is going on?"

We discover that the heater is broken and it is 41 degrees inside the house. We look around the house, and it is a dusty, neglected mess. This is going to be a long few weeks, and I can feel the tear factory waking up. I won't cry tonight, but I will be crying soon.

"What have we done?" Aaron and I look at each other. Then we turn to look at our daughter and two dogs. We are in for a very cold night.

We wake up the next day frozen and sluggish. There's more calamity to come.

Being at my mother's house requires a shift in routine with getting my daughter to school, so I drive her, and I am thankful for the car heater. I load the dogs in the back because they need to go to the groomer immediately. They are untouchable pincushions after rolling around in cockle burrs from Mom's unkempt backyard. I also need to get to work as the emails are rolling in fast and I have a business call in the next few minutes.

I find myself looking for the comfort of normalcy. My family members have turned into popsicles from the cold house so we can barely think straight. Our house closing is upon us, and we still have an outstanding item that is holding us up. A contractor agreed to repair the soffit on our house, and it was required that we have the estimate and a check before we could close. We have one hour to go, and we haven't heard from him. We may not be able to close today.

Now, I am a hot mess of chaos. A head explosion is coming to the surface.

"Calgon, take me away!"

My eyes start watering as I pull cockle burrs out of my sweater, and I start praying out loud in the nice warm car. I find myself speaking scriptures out loud to calm myself, like

"God is not the author of confusion!" and "No weapon formed against me shall prosper!" This is my way of getting all these irritating loose ends tied up and under control as those annoying tears surface.

Five minutes later as I am sobbing alone on the side of the road, things suddenly start falling into place. The contractor's estimate comes through so that I can get the cashier's check. I head to the bank, get everything squared away, and go to close on the house as I wipe my eyes. The deal is done, the dogs are groomed, and someone is coming to fix the heater. Thank you, Jesus!

Miracles happen, but I recognize that I need to plan for the next time Murphy's Law comes to visit me again.

3 Things to Put into Practice When You Experience Calamity and Chaos

Composing your soul doesn't happen in an instant. You have to develop it in small increments, and simply force yourself to embrace it. I emphasize the word *force* because it doesn't come to you naturally; you have to go after it. There are three ways to initiate composure when calamity comes to town and you are threatened with chaos:

1. **Have a strategy:** Before calamity happens, know that chaos will try to follow it. Intentionally build peace into your future. Envision how you will be composed when turmoil arises. Picture yourself calmly reacting when you meet calamity, noting that you will not be inviting chaos into your life today.

2. **Step away:** Cut chaos off at the pass. When it appears, stop what you are doing and just be quiet and breathe.

A simple, yet powerful exercise is to go outside, sit, and look up at the sky as you breathe deeply.

3. **Practice the Law of Replacement:** As you plan your strategy, apply this formula:

When you take away X, then it must be replaced by Y so that you will get Z.

Think about what X, Y, and Z are for you. When you remove a behavior or reaction, you have to replace it with something else—ideally something more positive. Z is the result you want to get.

So if you know you in times of calamity you tend to become fatalistic (X), then you want to replace it with a different reaction of asking yourself curious questions (Y), which will give you a more peaceful disposition (Z).

Exercise: Apply the XYZ Formula

1. Journal about a calamity that you've experienced. What was your (X)? (The behavior or mindset you took on that you didn't want to have)?
2. What do you want to replace it with (Y)?
3. What is the outcome you expect to get (Z)?

Applying the formula helps to disrupt your negative thinking pattern and funnel the energy into a more productive process for you. The goal is to create a new neuro-pathway as you learn to process your situations differently.

Take time to think through this thoroughly. Just throwing out a random action isn't going to stick. For example, if you say, "I'm going on a diet tomorrow," think about the obstacles you will encounter and what your plan of attack will be. Decide what values you will honor and how you will shut down inner critics. If you don't invest in the plan, you won't stick to it. This will create a failure cycle for you, and your inner critics will beat you up over it.

Speaking of productive processes, I want to get more in depth with you about composing your soul in the next chapter by working on your perspective.

CHAPTER 11

PRACTICE WITH A TRAINING DAY PERSPECTIVE

"God keeps telling me to count it all joy when tough days happen. I should be the happiest person on this planet!" -Angie Nuttle

What happens when you have a difficult and stressful day? More importantly, what happens *to you* when you go through a tough day?

I don't know of anyone who says, "Wow! I really loved having this tough day, and I enjoyed feeling tense and uncertain!"

We rightfully get overwhelmed and stressed when the day's calamities overtake us. It's not helpful to ignore or pretend like it isn't difficult, but we can reframe what a stressful, challenging day is, and how you can take care of yourself differently.

Let's start with *perspective*: Instead of thinking of it as a difficult day, see it as a Training Day.

Composing your soul takes resilience-building. We can't build resilience if we don't get a workout, right? It's just like going to the gym.

You don't just go in, stand around and watch other people work out. If you want to get in shape, you have to get in there, get your cardio on, and pump some iron.

You sweat. You get sore. You are creating micro-tears in your muscles so they can heal and create firm scar tissue. The next time you go to the gym, it's a little less painful. You've built resilience and gotten into better shape. And you plan for the next time you need to train.

Dealing with a stressful day or time period is similar. You may not be able to control everything that is happening, but you can prepare yourself for how you will take care of yourself before, during, and after the experience. Very much like the *3 steps to deal with calamity and chaos* strategy I mentioned in the last chapter.

Let's move into a story to understand the Training Day concept.

STORY: The Training Day

Recently, I had one of the most intense training days I've had in many years. I had taken on a client that I had worked with before and knew that it took a lot of energy to manage them. The CEO, a gentleman that I really appreciated, was desperate for my help. I agreed to do a short contract to provide HR support until we could implement a permanent solution for them, and I put three contractors on the project. Here's my recollection:

I can see the storm brewing.

Six weeks into the contract, one of my contractors is out for a week due to a pre-planned event, and it falls on a payroll week. She agrees to run payroll remotely, and it will be the first one by herself. There is a passing concern that the payroll system run by a vendor has some quirky gaps, but it is felt that everything will work out fine.

There's a thundercloud on the horizon figuratively speaking. Another contractor isn't meshing well with the client and is struggling with responsiveness. Another problem to deal with.

The situation leaves me picking up a lot of extra work until my other contractor can return, and I am already loaded down with other client work. I manage to keep my head together knowing that we are working toward the permanent solution that will allow us to finish this project. Still, the storm is building momentum.

Training Day arrives. It's Friday at 7:30 a.m. and the client calls, frantically relaying that the hourly staff only got paid half of their checks. Some people didn't even get a check, and everyone is pissed off. We are in full crisis mode.

Panicky emails start flying, and phone calls are coming in. Emotions are so palpable as the CEO demands the situation be fixed immediately.

Within a few minutes, we discover that the payroll vendor is responsible for the debacle, but my client CEO is pointing the finger at us. He is angry and panicked. We needed to a) get the payroll corrected immediately, and b) manage the client and our reputation.

I cancel all of my morning appointments as I feel my fight or flight stress response kick in. It's that familiar jolt of electric shock chemicals running through my body as I work to compose my plan. *Executive Coach* shows up in the driver's seat of my inner committee.

Take 5 minutes to compose yourself.

She is calming me and activating something I call the 4 Personal Pillars (Physical, Emotional, Spiritual, and Mental). I begin operating in them:

1. I step outside and take deep cleansing breaths (Physical).
2. I become aware of the feelings I am experiencing (fear, anxiety) (Emotional).
3. I pray about the situation (Spiritual).
4. I shut down my inner critics and speak positive words into the situation (Mental).

Now that I am calm and more mentally flexible, I jump back in. So does *Crisis Manager.*

I bring everyone together for an emergency conference call to triage the situation and establish a solution-focused dialogue. We are waiting for one of my contractors to get on the call and give us an update, so I encourage everyone to speak out loud about what is happening. Having the conversation is powerful medicine to calm the air.

BBBGRRRRIINNNNNGGGGGG!

A loud shrieking noise suddenly stops our conversation as the fire alarm goes off in one of the company locations. We quickly end the call so that everyone can exit the building. We agree that we will jump back on in a few minutes. Our momentum is temporarily interrupted.

I repeat the 4 Personal Pillars while waiting. Just having the structure of it creates a sense of sanity, and it allows *Executive Coach* to work with me internally.

Back on the call now, my contractor gives us good news, and the employees will be getting an off-cycle direct deposit. We know that the problem originated from the vendor, but I can tell the CEO isn't convinced, so we agreed to do an "after accident review" with the vendor later in the week.

For now, the crisis is squashed, and I am facing a solidly booked calendar of coaching calls. I also have one unpleasant task at the end of the day: releasing one of my contractors from the project. It goes smoothly in spite of the difficult situation, and I move on with a big sigh of relief.

The Cool Down and Recovery: Aftermath of the Training Day

The composure of my soul had to be thoughtfully sprinkled throughout the day. After a day like this, I knew I would need to continue my self-care to cool down. The 4 Personal Pillars had been good to me, so I chose to continue on that path. Here's the rest of the story:

My family is out of town for a short excursion, so I have the place to myself. The call of wine enters my head, but I quickly decide that I don't want to numb myself (and feel yucky later). I need to take care of myself thoughtfully.

When I get home, I recognize a familiar feeling in my body. It is the physical feeling of homesickness. The last time I had this feeling, I was 10. I revisit that experience.

My mom went into fast labor with my youngest sister, and I was dropped off at a stranger's house for two days, not knowing what was happening. The people were very nice, but I still had a constant headache and struggled to eat anything because of the anxiety churning in my stomach. When my dad finally picked me up two days later, brought me home, and fed me a TV dinner, I instantly felt better.

When I come back from the memory, I think it is kind of odd. That the same feeling is physical and present in my body now. Nobody is home. I am alone. I have a gnawing in my stomach and head that has worn me out during the day.

I chose to take a brisk walk with the dogs. The walk is refreshing, and I can feel the physical toxicity working its way out of me. Afterward, I process what has helped me overcome that yucky feeling in the past. No, I don't want to run out and get a TV dinner. I've long outgrown that level of sentimentality.

I am now craving soup, hot tea, and calmness. My mind is flooded with thoughts of when I was younger, eating soup after suffering a tough bout of the flu or a nasty cold. I decide to hop into my car and head to a local Japanese restaurant.

The place is quaint and quiet. As I sip my soup and tea slowly, I can feel my heart rate returning to normal. I find it easier to breathe, and my body starts to relax. I am healing.

Just like the micro-tears in muscles when a workout is done, the body starts to repair itself when it gets rest. I am now in recovery mode from Training Day, and The 4 Personal Pillars are successfully partnering with me to work through it.

On this night, I sleep like a baby.

Exercise: Reflection on Your Past Training Day Patterns

In your journal, reflect on some of your tough days from the past. Respond to the following questions:

1. What patterns do you notice about yourself as you go through a training day?
2. What coping mechanism do you usually rely on?
3. Are your coping mechanisms effective?
4. In what ways do you struggle to cope in a way that is healthy?
5. How do you take care of yourself after a training day (if at all)?

CHAPTER 12

THE POWER OF THE 4 PERSONAL PILLARS

"Who wants advice from somebody who isn't walking the talk? Not me. All my role models better be taking care of themselves before they try to help me."
-Angie Nuttle

As you see in the Training Day story from the last chapter, you can think about composing your soul four ways:

- Physically
- Spiritually
- Emotional
- Mentally

These components of your soul are deeply integrated and work together like a car tire. If they are balanced, the wheel will move on the pavement smoothly and get you to your destination. You will still encounter bumps and potholes, but your resilience to them will be at a higher level. If one of these components is lacking, the wheel starts to go flat, and any obstacle in the road will put you at risk for a blowout.

Each pillar has multiple aspects, so I will focus on a few select topics for each one. Let's examine each component's meaning, relevance, and impact at a deeper level.

PHYSICAL PILLAR

Have you ever noticed that when you exercise, it is like a dam is broken and overflows in your mind? You are killing it all day long at work, and you unexpectedly hit a wall. You jump on the treadmill or go for a run, and your thinking suddenly comes back online. It's a beautiful occurrence.

How about when you when you are eating healthy? You seem to be more clear in your thinking. You process thoughts faster. Conversely, when you overeat at the fried chicken and apple pie buffet, how do you feel afterward? Sluggish, tired, and regretful and the words that come to mind, right?

In this day and age, it's extremely popular in society to be active and fit, and for good reasons. Your eating habits and food choices certainly impact your overall physiological being, which influences how you feel each day.

It also impacts your biological functions and how well you process thinking. Your movements and physical exertion have a chemical effect on you and work toxins out of your body when you practice it daily.

You have control over all of this.

The discipline of taking care of your body through eating right and exercising leads to optimal health, but one of the most important physical actions you can take is to sleep. When you sleep, you are allowing your physical being and neurological functions to process the day's activities. Your brain during sleep might sound something like this:

Brain to body parts: "Hey, looks like we had a heck of a day. Who needs repair services?

Arm: "I do. I fell today, and I am broken."

Brain: "Okay, this is a priority. All crisis troops report to the Arm for healing triage. Those left, let's assess our memory function. We had a lot of neurotransmitters activated today. What memories do we need to keep and which ones need to be let go?"

You get the point. Most of the work done to our physical being happens when you sleep. If you aren't allowing yourself enough time, it's just like being in a job where the deadlines are short on a regular basis, and you burn out. You go into survival mode, which doesn't allow your body parts to do their best. This eventually leads you to break down. You don't function as well; your thinking becomes less clear. Your immunity opens its gates wide for every virus and disease to come in and jack up your physical operation.

You have control over your physical being. It's a matter of you choosing the right path to move toward healing and healthiness.

STORY: From Physical Failure to Victory

I put significant energy into my work in corporate America for over 20 years. In my last few years there, my health suffered greatly. I was always sick, caught every flu bug that flew by, and my weight steadily increased. Even when I tried to diet with my previously successful high protein/low carb, it just wasn't working. I tried to start walking, but I wasn't consistent.

At one point, I was traveling 70% of my working time, and I became an emotional eater to temporarily comfort my desire to be home with my family. My sleep suffered, and I was getting about 4 to 5 hours per night. I spent the waking hours pushing more work, and I let the work come first. I had a ton of Training Days.

Physically, I felt terrible and drained. I went to doctors, and at one point, they thought I might have Lupus. The cycle of physical abuse to myself had led me down a path where my body was controlling me, instead of me controlling it. Then in 2013, I had two car accidents right in a row, both from texters who weren't paying attention to the road and ran into me.

It was the best thing that could have happened to me.

Why? Because it took me on a new journey of getting my health back. The accidents left my back in terrible shape and unbearable pain. I went to numerous doctors who kept loading me up with high-powered medicines, but I wasn't able to find a healthy solution. For months, I wore a back brace, and my mind was so foggy that it took extra energy to get through the workday. I struggled to walk anywhere for longer than 10 minutes. I was eating more junk to comfort myself, which led me further down a physically destructive path.

I felt like I was aging rapidly, and dying.

After a series of unproductive medical doctor visits and a boatload of money, I found my way to a unique health and wellness clinic. The chiropractic care is what drew me in, and the doctor there was an upper cervical specialist. At the time, I didn't believe in alternative holistic treatments, but after a complete assessment, and the way I was feeling, I didn't have anything to lose. I agreed to a full treatment plan of holistic treatment and alternative medicine.

Within two weeks, I started getting better. My choice to finally take care of my body allowed me to begin healing from all the corporate abuse I had subjected myself to. I was also able to drop 23 pounds, get a healthy glow back on my face, and walk for up to 60 minutes without back pain.

It took a solid year to regain my health. Thanks to the help and dedication of The Prather Practice in Indianapolis, I continue to thrive today.

In summary, the impact of care for your physical health comes from you making the decision to take care of yourself. This involves a strategy of having a healthy daily diet, physical exercise, and allowing your body to recover when you put pressure on it to perform. You already know this, but you may be struggling to implement a plan.

What could be in your way?

You have to really want it. Getting healthy has to be so important that you are willing to discipline your mind and put in the work. But, you are probably having struggles with one of the other pillars, and that's why you haven't been able to stick with a plan for long periods of time.

Each pillar feeds into the other, and each one influences the others. They are like partners, remember? Take a moment to reflect.

EXERCISE: Physical Pillar Reflection

- How would you rate the strength of your physical pillar on a scale of 1-10, 10 being perfect?
- What do you struggle with the most: eating, sleeping, working, exercising, or other health components?
- What's the one thing you know you need to address now?
- What are you choosing to value?

EMOTIONAL PILLAR

Napoleon Dynamite.

When I think of this movie, I feel joy. There is a laugh in my soul. I love the simplicity of the storyline and its characters. Napoleon has a knack for being impacted by Murphy's Law, being misunderstood, but getting through all that to become the hero at the end. I could be his sister.

The power of emotion causes us to be drawn to movies, to listen intently to beautiful songs, and to fall in love. Its power can also lead us to fight a wrong, lash out at someone who's hurt us, and sob when we've lost a loved one. We look for commonality with people, places, and things so that we can feel normal and understood.

We desire to relate, and we make our decisions based on how we feel. This is proven by Richard Damasio's research. He and other researchers note that at least 80% of our decisions are emotionally based whether we want to admit it or not. This means we have the power to get our emotional health flowing in the right direction.

The emotional pillar takes continual nurturing by practicing everything that I have talked about up to this point. You've learned that pre-existing conditions act as filters for your personal view. You've learned about your triggers and emotional composure. You put a lot of energy into expressing and suppressing raw emotions. You also know about the roles you operate in, and how to practice ESP to desensitize them.

Emotions are healthy and deserve the chance to live outside of you. You can strengthen your pillar by allowing yourself to be authentic and expressive, but also by practicing the art of composure. This is where self-discipline and choice are critical to your success.

The Truth about Emotions and Alcohol

I want to highlight another topic: Your emotions and alcohol. I believe your emotions are the biggest culprit in its use, yet popular advice leads us to turn to alcohol as a soothing salve.

- You've gotten a promotion, so of course; you've got to celebrate with champagne.
- Your grandma passed away. Have a drink to downplay your emotions. "It's good medicine."
- You need to relax, so have some wine. (My personal favorite.)

My position on alcohol is that it is not evil, nor is it the answer for everything. It's how you use it that is the challenge. I really enjoy a glass of wine. However, I have to watch it when I am going through stressful times because I struggle to stop at one. It's easy to turn it into a substitute for working through challenges and can become a habit before you know it.

We are constantly on the continuum of pleasure and pain, so when we feel pain, we immediately want a remedy. Alcohol will call your name and pretend to be your friend.

Alcohol is tricky because it provides a temporary suppression of our pain and stress, telling us that we now feel relaxed. It causes us to be sluggish, and it is like sludge in our brains. Can it release inhibitions? Definitely. Can it make us do and say stupid things? Absolutely. You see it all the time on Facebook. When you mix alcohol with Facebook, you may wake up the next day being unfriended by several people.

Over time, continued use of alcohol to express or suppress emotions has shown to cause neurological changes. A study cited by Time Magazine revealed that regular drinkers process emotions differently than nondrinkers. Massachusetts General Hospital and the *Journal of Alcoholism: Clinical and*

Experimental Research showed that nondrinkers process emotions in their amygdala, and drinkers' emotions' are processed in their prefrontal cortex. The significance of this is that the amygdala is designed to recognize a threat and sound the alarm. The pre-frontal cortex is the judge of whether the alarm is justified or not. Chronic use of alcohol interrupts the relationship between the two parts of the brain, so drinkers have a harder time processing and regulating their emotions.

The results also showed that that drinkers tend to misinterpret nonverbal cues and facial expressions, leading to off-target assumptions and responses. They are also more aggressive and less inhibited. So, you can probably go to your local bar and see this happening without the study results. The point is that alcohol can become a brain wrecking ball that will have you misreading people and getting angry for no reason.

The truth is that alcohol isn't a friend at all. It pretends to take care of you but leaves you holding the emotional baggage that you are trying to get rid of.

STORY: The Facebook Friend Request

My mom had back surgery and was struggling with some side effects. She developed balance issues, and the family was concerned about her.

My aunt and uncle came by one day to visit with her. I was headed out to a client meeting, so I left them to chat it up for the afternoon.

When I returned that evening, Mom was on the couch with an ice pack on her head. She had fallen and had a goose egg on the back of her head. I was concerned and recommended that we go to the emergency room, but she insisted she was fine and coherent. I kept an eye on her that evening, and she seemed to be okay.

On my way to bed, a close relative texted to see how Mom was. The relative had a sensitive personality and also drank frequently. Based on the text, the relative seemed to be indulging. I let the relative know that Mom was fine and not to worry. I shut my phone off and forgot about it as I dozed off into a wonderful sleep. Two days later, here's my recollection:

I am having coffee with Mom and easing into the day. She's feeling fine, and we are doing a devotional time together. I open my computer, check out the inspirational posts on Facebook, and see something odd. It's a It's a friend request from the relative.

"We are obviously connected already. I wonder if this is a hacker. Let me email to double check."

I instant message her about the friend request.

"Hey there, I got a friend request from you. Is this real or is it a hacker?"

She immediately responds.

"Yeah. It's from me."

I am puzzled. I have had half a cup of coffee. Maybe I am not getting it.

"Okay. How did we get disconnected?"

I am sensing something weird now. She's thinking, then she types.

"It was all a misunderstanding. I am fine now."

I am stunned. I have absolutely no clue what this means. I decide to dig deeper.

"I'm not clear, misunderstanding? What are you talking about?"

I wait for about 5 minutes as she responds. I can tell she is struggling for words. Here's the truncated version of what she says:

"I thought you abandoned your mom after she had a fall and hit her head. I was worried about her and tried calling but couldn't reach you, and I thought you were ignoring me. I called her, and she said she was fine, but she wasn't fine, and she said you were gone. I tried calling you and Aaron, but nobody would answer. I found out later that you weren't even there when she fell, and it was someone else who was there. I am sorry, I got it all mixed up. I realize now that you didn't know about anything that was going on."

This is just nuts. I look at my phone, and the only time I see the relative contacting me is that late night text. I also find out that the relative got the whole family spun up and they were calling my husband's work phone thinking it is my number. He rarely checks those messages, so all my relatives are thinking I am just not being responsive and not caring about my mom. An emotional trigger around responsiveness has just been set off.

I start to feel some heat rise in my neck as I process this trial and execution that has been happening without my knowledge. The relative has:

1. Misread and misinterpreted the entire situation.
2. Created a fictional story in her head.
3. Decided that I had done something bad without consulting with anyone; and
4. Published it to the world.

My Punishment? I have been sentenced to Facebook Unfriendship. Wow.

The truth is that my relative does this sort of thing regularly when she is drinking. She overreacts, misreads people, and gets depressed over the strangest things. She is processing from her pre-frontal cortex instead of her amygdala, so it's harder for her to regulate her emotions and perceptions. She always feels like she is being wronged and creates stories in her head. When she sobers up, she eventually comes to her senses and realizes her errors. She is remorseful, and she wants immediate reconciliation because she values harmony.

It is a fascinating example that shows the kamikaze effects of alcohol and emotions.

Well, I admit that I am angry about this, so I let her know that I am very disappointed about everything. I am fighting to get myself out of Child mode, and there is a part of me that wants to continue to throw a fit. I recognize it, and I know I can't take action right now until I cool down.

I decide to wait all day, and I entertain Child mode a little bit longer. I eventually regain my composure by thinking through the E.S.P. tool so I can switch to Adult mode.

After concluding that forgiveness is the best policy, I finally accept her friend request. I also send out a neutral and informational family memo with my correct number so they can contact me anytime they need to.

The experience leaves me grateful for this powerful example that I can share with others about the relationship between alcohol and emotions. Every experience is useful.

Exercise: Emotional Pillar Reflection

- What areas of your life do you believe your emotional pillar is strong?
- What are some areas in which your emotional pillar gets shaky?
- What's your perspective about alcohol and emotions?
- Is there an action you need to take?

MENTAL PILLAR

The act of cognitive processing is at the center of the mental pillar. While the emotional pillar is about expression, the mental pillar is about clear thinking as you face the complexities in your environment. Remember when I talked about your written code and the MBTI? This is where that all fits in.

All of the other pillars are connected and have a significant impact on this one. For example, think about a time you lost a loved one. Your emotions were put into overdrive because you were reacting to that experience. It was probably harder to think through what you needed to do or focus on your work. Your mental processing was temporarily hindered or slower than usual because of those strong emotions.

You may have also experienced a drop in physical energy. Your crisis chemicals were kicking in, and your internal emergency response team showed up to provide support for your emotional state. This required more fuel, so it took from your stash of energy, leaving your mental pillar with less energy to operate smoothly.

You may have tried to take some kind of action to soothe your mental state, like:

- Take a hot shower
- Sit outside quietly
- Listen to chimes
- Take a brisk walk
- Go to the bookstore
- Watch a thunderstorm

Eventually, you came back to a place of balance, and you were able to get into the swing of things. You returned to work and could continue as you resolved your emotional state. It's the template of those neural pathways that got you back into your routine so you could carry on as you were before.

As you build a healthy mental pillar, it's important to look at the things that distract you. If you are in a constant state of interruption, you will start to break down your well-oiled machine. This is a busy world, and you know you have to discipline yourself to focus if you want to keep the machine running. Here are a few research facts about distractions and their impact:

- According to a UC Irvine study, the average person is interrupted every 11 minutes, and it takes 25 minutes to return to where they were in their mental processing.
- *The Journal of Stress Management* found that people who are frequently interrupted experienced a 10% increase in exhaustion rates.
- *The Journal of Experimental Psychology* found that interruptions increased a person's need to speed up, causing an increase in stress and up to 4 times more task errors.

Basically, distractions can lower your productivity, cost you money, and drive you crazy. What's the best way to establish mental clarity? Reduce distractions and interruptions.

STORY: The Hallway of Distractions

Part of my business involves keeping my blogs current, writing my marketing content, and creating material for my workshops. According to my natural algorithm, mornings are my best time for writing, thinking, and capturing ideas. Mornings are also the most likely time that an interruption will occur.

I was working on a writing project and was struggling to create the content. This went on for several days. Ideas would pop in my head, but I always found myself getting caught up in something else.

The dogs would come into my office and tear something up. The hubby would come flying down the stairs with a contact lens emergency, needing my help. The kiddo had a new invention that she needed to discuss. I would lose valuable thoughts because I wasn't able to concentrate on getting them written. I was entering a place of major frustration, and my mental pillar was not firing on all cylinders.

One morning after I had finished up my reflection time, the inspiration was back. I decided to head straight to my office to get the content in a Word document. I was determined to get it down this time without any interruptions. Here's my recollection:

I am heading from the study to the office, and I sit down at the computer. I see that several people have emailed me based on the bold black font calling my name in the email box.

Let me take just a minute to respond back to a couple of these.

It's my need to be responsive that's telling me just to take care of these people. I want to get these emails off my plate so I can completely focus. I attempt to stop myself.

"No! I have plenty of time today to answer these emails. The world will not end if I don't answer right now."

I breathe, then start to open my document. My daughter walks in at that very moment. She's up an hour early.

"I don't feel good, Mommy." I guess I need to turn my attention to her. Darn it!

It is clear to me that the inspirational thought is not going to happen at that moment. My mind goes to deep space. I envision myself walking down a hallway, trying to get through the door at the end of it, only to be sucked in by all the doors along the hallway that serve to distract me. The doors have names:

Door 1: "Your email is calling your name."
Door 2: "You've got to keep on top of things."
Door 3: "You've got to be ultra-responsive."
Door 4: "You've got to get Tylenol and breakfast for your kid."

Then there is a door at the end of the hall. It says, "You've got to capture your inspirational thought."

I come back from deep space to see my daughter standing in front of me, disheveled hair, and a cringing look of pain. My obvious priority is to get her situated, but I am determined to get to that door at the end of the hallway soon. I will not let the distractions derail me. So, I fix her breakfast, give her Tylenol, then I sit down with my laptop while she's eating. I begin typing and manage to capture a few lines.

As usual, the dogs have to be near me at all times. They are under the table playing and barking. As they are playing, they start skidding on the floor and stabbing my feet with their claws.

Another door appears in my head: "Manage the dogs."

I decide I can't handle it, so I move to the sunroom. The moment I sit down, both neighbors begin cutting their grass, as if they had planned it at that exact moment. Judging from the loud buzz saw sound, another neighbor is cutting down a tree somewhere in the distance.

Really? It isn't even 7:30 yet! This has got to be a conspiracy.

I head back toward the kitchen when I notice there is a trail of something on the floor. What is this? I am compelled to investigate. I follow the trail, and it leads to the laundry room, where I find smashed dog poop in front of the dryer. I conclude with certainty that Mackenzie has stepped in it and tracked it through the house. Another door has been created called "Clean up the dog poop." Will I ever get to the door at the end of the hallway?

Now I am the one who is barking. I feel a head explosion arriving, and it exits my mouth.

"UUUUUUGGGGGGGGGGGHHHHHHHH!!!!!!!!!!!!!!!!!!!" (Yes, I expressed it with all caps, long and stretched out with a lot of exclamation points.)

My mental pillar is toppling. I have so many mental processes going on at this moment; it's like too many open windows on the desktop. Finally, the computer crashes. My screen has gone blank for a minute. Everything is gray.

My mind reboots, and my inner committee shows up. I realize that Murphy's Law has snuck into the driver's seat and I am completely annoyed by the discombobulation he has created.

I call forth Crisis Manager, who steps in to take over the cleanup of this big mess. She orders the dogs put in their crates, and the kiddo to help clean up the floor. She brings an idea to capture the inspirational thought on the iPhone notes, so it isn't lost. I can see her holding up the idea like a hero. She is trying to save it from drowning.

Once it is all taken care of, she orders me to go outside. Executive Coach takes over.

"Breathe. Slow down. Look up at the sky. Regain your composure. Allow your heart rate to return to normal. Take care of yourself in this moment."

I feel my soul begin to calm down. It's like a light snow falling on the ground in late fall. The tiny snowflakes are banding together to cool the ground, covering it with one clean sheet. It is a fresh start with new hope. I am officially cooling down, and it feels soothing.

Madam CEO shows up and wants to do some strategic planning to prevent this from happening again. She wants action and results. Executive Coach is there too and encourages me to put on a curious hat. She asks:

"What got in your way?"

I begin processing, and the list comes to mind:

- The feeling that I HAVE TO respond immediately.
- The belief that I need to "clear the table" of emails first, to accomplish my goal.
- Unexpected interruptions that are not planned for.
- A constant self-talk over several days that says, "You can do this later."
- Putting myself last over and over.

Inner critics have added fuel to the fire, like *Should-Ann,* who could be heard saying:

"Now you know you should stop focusing on yourself and your needs so you can make sure everyone else is taken care of. Get over there and take care of your kid you negligent parent. And clean up that dog poop. How did you let this happen? Shame on you!"

I have allowed all of these things to serve as gatekeepers to me accomplishing something that I want to do, and need to do. Note that I said, *"I allowed . . . "* With the exception of my daughter getting up an hour early, all other distractions could have been stopped or prevented if I would have:

- Established personal boundaries
- Planned ahead for distractions and interruptions
- Recognized the distractors when they showed up
- Prepared myself to combat them in general

These four steps seem simple; I just need to sit down and figure them out, which means an investment of more time. I have the power to clear my calendar if this is that important to me. I conclude that it is time to take care of me. To fill other people's buckets, I need to fill my own, so I can have the energy to help them.

What is the plan?

1. Set a boundary of not opening email when I am about to do something important.
2. Put the dogs up before I need to do something important.
3. Put a sign on my door: "Do not enter unless there is a fire or medical emergency," then lock the door.
4. When I get up, have my daughter's breakfast ready for her, or have her get it herself.
5. Talk with the family about my boundaries and request that they honor them unless there is a true emergency.
6. Block time for me and stick to it.
7. Go on vacation.

I begin implementing the plan, and although there is a little bit of pushback, I stick to my guns. A powerful lesson has been learned: The universe (and people) will respect your boundaries and mental processes when you start respecting them yourself.

Exercise: Mental Pillar Reflection

- What mental processes are you putting on the back burner in order to accommodate everything and everyone else?
- Think about your life. What does your Hall of Distractions look like, and what is the door at the end symbolize to you?
- Where do you need to establish boundaries?

SPIRITUAL PILLAR

The spiritual pillar relates to the intangible or nonphysical things that impact us.

I saved this pillar for last because when you've worked through all the other ones, things still happen that cannot be explained by science. You can lead a healthy lifestyle, express your emotions eloquently, and manage your mental processes with brilliance. There is simply . . . something else out there.

These pillars won't stop the world from operating, the collection of taxes from the government, and the occurrence of unexplained events like miracles and disasters. When you discover that you don't have control over the whole universe, it can be scary.

Some believe in serendipity. Some believe in Jesus. Others have a different god with a different name, while others refuse to believe in anything at all. Some mysteries can't be explained. And then there are revelations that strike people in a way that their perspectives are changed forever.

People search for deeper truths and understanding through church, reading, yoga, meditation, mindfulness, prayer, worship, drugs, experiences; the list is endless. The truth is that there is an entity beyond what we see within our five senses.

When we become aware of something spiritual, its presence is powerful and life changing. We tend to seek it most when times get tough, and when we face circumstances that we have no control over. Just like in the Boat Miracle Story I shared with you.

Think of the times you dealt with extremely difficult circumstances. A child in your family was critically ill, or a close friend was in a serious car accident. The news was not positive, and there was nothing else the doctors could do. Worse, there was nothing you could do. You felt a sense of desperation. Where did you turn?

When you are looking for answers and seeking hope, you create an open invitation to your soul. You may notice that you start receiving responses to your invitation. Change happens in the atmosphere. Maybe you felt a presence near you but didn't see anything. You heard something, but nothing was there. You saw something, but couldn't explain it.

You started to pray. You listened more intently for an answer and were inspired by song or poem. You were drawn to go into a deeper place of meaning. You were compelled to come up higher into an unfamiliar realm that seemed surreal, like a vision. You looked for the answer, and you got some kind of response because you tuned in.

People from all walks of life report spiritual experiences that have changed their lives. They choose to tune in for the answer by practicing some form of spiritual exercise. What is the purpose? To compose their souls.

In a survey I conducted recently, I asked people how they operate best, and what methods they use to overcome difficult circumstances. Here are a few responses I received:

- *Shelley Hoke, Healthcare Equipment*: "Meditation, exercise, music, calls to family and friends."
- *Claudia Womble, Federal Government*: "I pray every day that my work will glorify His Excellence."
- *Miriam Ferguson, Hospital Healthcare*: "1. My faith and going to the Lord in prayer is my first step. It reminds me what is truly important. 2. Listening to music, especially praise music. It helps provide balance and encouragement. "

Whatever it is that shows up, it works to compose souls and enrich lives. We climb higher to gain a different perspective at a 50,000-foot level, we allow our vulnerability to be known as we admit our helplessness, and we feel a sense of release as we receive answers.

STORY: The Grateful Encounter That Changed My Life

This is a very personal story that has changed the trajectory of my life. I am fully crossing the line from Corporate Talent Expert to a Christian who believes in a higher power. For me to live authentically, I must share this part of my life because it is the underpinning of my mission. It has led me to work with thousands of people like you who deserve to be seen, heard, valued, and celebrated, no matter who you are and where you have been.

I am taking you back to the summer of 1994, the year I graduated with my Bachelor's degree. The accomplishment was memorable in so many ways. To give you some context, I was the first woman in my family to get this far in school, so it was a big deal.

No one believed that I would be successful or even alive long enough to get a degree. My early years brought tremendous pain. I was viewed as an unruly rebel, which was salt to my open wounds. I was bitter and angry.

To cope with the rejection, I became a rebellious smart-mouth who learned to be street wise. I was compelled to leave the state of Indiana because I knew I would die there if I didn't. As soon as I turned 17, I hitchhiked from Indiana to Alabama so I could start my life fresh.

I can look back and see that something was drawing me to Alabama.

On the road, I was met with experiences that I rarely speak of, because they would frighten the people I love. Somehow I managed to get through them. My survival can be attributed to the fact that I sought God when I was in danger and had nobody else to turn to. Other times, I wrestled with Him, asking Him why this was happening. I also talked to Him when I was lonely, which was often.

I eventually married and had two children in Alabama. My husband's drug addiction left us chronically poor in spite of me working all the time. When I made the decision to go to school a few years later, I knew I had to do it because my young babies' survival was squarely on my shoulders.

Something else was tugging at me though. What was I being called to do? I could not put my finger on it just yet.

The four- year journey was the trial of my life. It was a hard and suffering path. My inner critics found their way to me through my husband's voice, who constantly tried to dissuade me from completing school. He fought me so hard that on the day of my last exam, he threw my keys out into the yard during a severe lightning storm. I would not be stopped, so I ran out, found the keys and left. With a mud stained pink sweat suit and soaking wet hair, I drove the hour trip to Troy, Alabama, took my exam as I sobbed, and passed with flying colors.

Although I was able to get loans and a Pell Grant, I still struggled with money. I learned to be creative and resourceful by exchanging babysitting time with a college friend. Every day, I would walk up the big hill of Troy State University with two babies in carriers, drop them off with my friend, go to classes, then pick up all the kids afterward and babysit. By the end, I was half starved, sleep deprived, and had really toned arms.

I graduated. For the first time in my life, I felt a deep sense of gratitude toward God. He was the only one who was there with me in my worst moments. He made me an overcomer and a seasoned fighter. Here's my recollection of what happened one week after I graduated:

It's Sunday morning, and I think I am going to church today. I've been to the country church down the road a few times. The pastor is unengaging, and the congregation is deader than a doornail, but I don't care. I am going to thank God.

I arrive in my Sunday dress. I feel clear–headed and joyful. There's a pew midway up on the left, so I slip in there on the end. I am trying to hear what the preacher is saying, but he is rattling on with incoherent jabber as usual. Remember, I'm here to thank God.

After a while, it's time for the altar call. The music minister calls out hymn number 111; *I Surrender All*. We all chime in to sing it.

"All to thee my blessed Savior, all to thee I freely give . . .
I will ever love and trust Him, in his presence daily live . . .
I Surrender All . . . "

Suddenly, the words are inside me, causing my heart to beat hard. These words are speaking to me, and I mean every single one. I look around, and everyone else is looking bored and tired as they lifelessly mouth the words.

I continue to sing with heartfelt appreciation, and something catches my eye.

It's a brilliant light that is above me, and it is rapidly growing. There is a figure in the light holding His arms out. I can't see anything else but Him. Without speaking out loud, He is welcoming me. I feel such a sense of love and acceptance that it is indescribable.

I am sobbing so uncontrollably that I think my heart will burst. I feel Him around me, letting me know I am His completely. Just when I am about to explode and can't take anymore, I come back to the church pew, and people are staring at me.

It is weird because I can hear their thoughts.

"What is wrong with her?"

"She probably did something really bad; she needs to ask forgiveness."

"You know, her husband is abusive, and she has those two babies. Poor thing."

"She should be on her knees praying to God."

I don't care. I have met my maker, and He sees me, hears me, values me, and celebrates me.

In a moment's time, I have changed completely. Every burden that I ever felt has been lifted off of me, and I feel so light. There is a smile on my tear washed face. On this day in June, I am clean, and there is a warm feeling inside of me.

For the next three weeks, I am so peaceful that I don't speak. The world is a whole new place. I hear the songs of the birds, I see the hues of green and blue in leaves, and I see the good in people. It seems like I've experienced this before, but the memory isn't clear.

One day, I am riding in the truck with the family, and the memory resurfaces. I realize that I have met the voice that spoke to me so many years before at Christian Park. I feel like a big bubbling fountain of joy, and I am smiling.

Finally, my children's father says: "What is wrong with you? Why are you smiling? You have not talked in three weeks!"

Happiness and contentment rise to meet his exasperation.

"Nothing's wrong. I don't have anything to complain about anymore."

Even he sees it. I have gone from a smart-mouthed rebel to a calm and composed soul. One encounter with God and I have done an about face turn in my life. It cannot be explained by science, and I don't have any pictures to prove it. All I know is that one experience is the catalyst for my future, and it is my wake up call. I am being called to live a better life and do something meaningful.

We are *all* called to do something meaningful.

EXERCISE: Spiritual Reflection

- What is your perspective on the spiritual aspect of life?
- When your world is chaotic, where do you turn?
- What is the most impactful spiritual experience you've ever had?
- Where is there an opportunity for you to grow spiritually?
- Do you believe you are being called to do something meaningful?

Processing the 4 Personal Pillars

If I could boil down a list of to-dos around the four pillars, I would simplify it in four sentences:

1. Practice regular physical detoxification.
2. Express emotions with intelligence and composure.
3. Remove distractions for clear mental processing.
4. Come up higher to a deeper spiritual plane.

These four components go a long way in composing your soul. I've learned this for myself, and I am pretty hardheaded. I have looked for shortcuts and ways to get around all of the pillars. There is no shortcut. If you want to get into your personal eye of the storm and out of the damaging winds of the world, you have to take care of yourself physically, emotionally, mentally, and spiritually.

When you gain self-awareness around the pillars, you will be able to create a cadence around them through a personal strategic plan. Take the time to reflect on the questions I have posed to you.

Where actions are concerned, small doses work. In each pillar, identify a single step you can take to build strong health. Too many steps are a recipe for failure and disappointment so be gentle, yet firm with yourself.

You will see that as you gain strength in your pillars, you will begin to gain more clarity about your mission, and how you can impact others. Understanding your natural algorithm will give you pieces of your mission, but strong pillars will bring forth the crystal clearness you need to move into your mission.

And this is the true reason for learning soul composure: To answer the call of your mission. It will be the ride of your life.

CHAPTER 13

THE *STRATEGY* TO DEAL WITH *SELF-DEFEATING* TOXICITY

"When you say you can't, what you're really saying is that you won't, or you don't want to." -Angie Nuttle

It's time for the tough talk.

You may be your own worst enemy. See if you frequently catch yourself saying self-defeating things like:

- I can't.
- I tried, but it didn't work.
- He/she won't let me.
- Yes, I can do that. (Even if you don't have the time.)
- No, I don't have time. (Because you have overbooked yourself.)
- I should do that. (Although you don't want to.)
- I shouldn't do that. (Although you want to.)

There are some damaging words that come out of our mouths that shout, "I am a victim!" We are all susceptible to chronic self-abuse, and the wrong words can diminish our worth. I run across so many people who spend more energy defending their victim position with some of the phrases I mentioned. I can boldly say that they are choosing to stay in a personal prison even when the door is open to step out.

Be careful, or you are likely to end up with one of these toxic results:

1. If you frequently use the word *Can't,* note that it is a word that needs to be struck from your dictionary if you are going to have a composed soul. It presents you as helpless and prone to a victim mentality. People will see you as incapable.
2. If you are over-committing, you are setting yourself up for energy and performance failure. If you present yourself as a doormat, people will walk on you because you have not respected yourself.
3. If you are blaming others for your inability to do something, then it will stall your progress and growth. People are eventually repelled by complainers and blamers.

I have a big question for you to meditate upon:

What is more important, *operating with a composed soul, pleasing people, or avoiding something?*

Answering this question requires thought, and also a decision about how you will operate and what your principles will be. You have more control and power than you may like to admit. You don't have to allow your environment to control you because you are not a victim of the universe. Ultimately, you are choosing to value one thing over another.

What will you choose to value?

STORY: Catching "I Can Do It All" in the Act

"I really overdid it this time."

Heart palpitations, restless sleep, and physical illness have taken me over. I am facing a convergence of situations happening in my life, and it is all my doing.

My schedule is crammed full because I said yes to everything and everyone. I look at the calendar as I try to regulate my hyperventilation. Several business deliverables are calling for my attention at once.

"At this rate, I am going to be up all night every night."

My thought is interrupted by an instant message and a text at the same time. One is from a former colleague; another is from a family member. It's 8:00 p.m. on a Wednesday.

"Hi Angie, it's Rachel. Can you help me with an HR problem I am having? I don't know what to do."

"Angie, I need you to call me. I am about to get divorced, and I need to tell you what is happening. Can you help me?"

The hubby pushes open the door past my "Do not enter unless there is a fire or medical emergency" sign, and comes into the room as I am sitting at the computer. We are in the process of selling our primary residence, a rental property, and building a house. He wants to talk about details of all three of these.

I am now out of sorts, and I feel another head explosion coming. I need a vacation, from myself.

The kiddo trots in, along with three dogs. We are all in my 10X10-foot office now, and Mackenzie informs me I have to take her to cheerleading practice tomorrow during the time that I have a business call.

"Give me 5 minutes." I motion for everyone to scoot out of my home office.

What is my problem? It is the fact that I feel the need to help everyone, help them now and do it freely (and many times for free). My other problem is that I have made it okay for everyone to run over my boundaries and stomp on them. Executive Coach pops up, and asks the question:

"What are you valuing more, Angie?"

At first, I tell myself that I value a composed soul, but my actions have proven otherwise. I have not done anything to create the necessary boundaries for composure. Instead, I am choosing to please people by saying yes. I am also choosing to avoid something.

I don't want to be viewed as useless. I need to be needed. I am avoiding the guilt of leaving someone behind who needs my help. All of these things are trumping my desire to have a composed soul, and it is a direct conflict with many of my values. My crystal clear value is suffering low visibility; I am not operating in freedom. By disrespecting my own time, people are simply following suit.

Something must change. It's me. And I need to get back in alignment with my values. It's time to value soul composure so I can authentically help others in a way that is healthy for them and me. I decide I need a top 3 short-term emergency plan for the moment:

1. I choose not to respond to the texts tonight. I may choose to respond tomorrow.
2. I do need to talk to the hubby. The house situation is important.
3. I need to shift around my schedule and spread some things out so I can breathe this week.

I also recognize I need a longer-term strategy to overcome my "I Can Do It All" behavior, which has built up tremendous toxicity in me.

I choose to book some time on my calendar later in the month to work through a strategy. To prepare for it, I do a few things:

1. "Is this really needed and meaningful right now?" I write this on my computer to remind me to curb my calendar until I could create my strategy.
2. Before the strategy day, I will do a technology fast. No social media, phone texts, Snap Chat, computer, or anything.
3. I will take daily brisk walks with the dogs or go to the gym.
4. I will do a 21-day Restrictive Detox diet to clear my mind and body.

After 22 days, I am ready for my personal Strategy Day. I've been anticipating this like it was my birthday party.

Incredible is the only word I can think of that articulates how I feel on this day! I feel disciplined, clear, detoxified, and I already have a head start on my strategy. Knowing that I still need to go deeper, I dive into the day with bubbly and grateful enthusiasm.

Exercise: **Process Your Own Personal Experience**

We are going to pause here because I want you to process your own experience. Can you relate to the story I just shared? Maybe the circumstances are a little different, but you've found yourself overwhelmed and underappreciated. Focus on the big question I asked you, "What is more important, *operating with a composed soul, pleasing people, or avoiding something*? Take a moment to reflect on these questions:

- Think of the last time you desperately wanted something. What was it?
- What was your mindset like?
- How did you approach getting it?
- What were the obstacles?
- What was less important to you, and what was more important?
- What did the experience give you?

Once you complete these, continue on with your reading, and I will share what I did.

TOOL: The 4-Step Strategy to Get Rid of Self-Defeating Toxicity

By the time I finished my Strategy Day, I had created a 4-step strategy that aligned with my values, beliefs, and overall natural algorithm. I got very specific about the things that needed to change, and the steps I would take to move forward. I also prioritized everything, putting key reminders on my calendar so it could be embedded into my daily life. Then I hit the go button and activated my plan. After 3 months, I was able to see a major difference. I managed to:

- Give myself more dedicated space on my calendar
- Stop being so responsive in times when it isn't necessary
- Share and reinforce my boundaries with family (even though it's been painful for them)

Several changes started taking place, and I felt myself becoming much more in control of my time. I also felt better in all four of the personal pillars, especially when I did my detoxifying diet.

I am going to share the strategy template with you now so you can start planning your own Strategy Day. If you are really serious about being the best you and getting different results, do this.

The four steps are:

1. Release
2. Resist
3. Revive
4. Restore

Step I: Release

A great place to start is to view yourself as carrying around baggage. It's very heavy, and it is weighing you down. To rise above, the baggage has to be released. This is the toughest part because it's hard to let things go. The plan to change your future direction is most at risk to become lost here because of *unwillingness*. If you've ever watched the show, *Hoarders*, you can compare their struggle to this one. Those hoarders want to hold on to every bit of trash, even if rats and bugs are crawling all over it.

For those who genuinely want to move forward, a commitment must be made to release the things that are getting in the way of personal balance. These are various categories to analyze:

- Work Release (yes, it is a play on words but easy to remember- problems at work)
- Unhealthy Relationships

- Toxic Emotional Responses (unforgiveness, passive aggressiveness, withdrawal)
- Physical Clutter and "Stuff"
- Behavioral Habits (race car driving in rush hour traffic, cursing at people, yelling)
- Unproductive Thinking Patterns (excessive judging, fatalism)
- Physical Abuse of Self (alcohol, unhealthy eating and sleep habits, driving self too hard)

For each of the categories, answer these three questions:

1. What do I need to release or let go of?
2. What do I need to replace it with?
3. What result will this give me?

Step 2: Resist

As you work through the processing of releasing, you know that those habits and behaviors have been etched in your brain. You have created neuro-pathways that need to be rewritten, and you want to find ways to resist falling into the same rut you were in.

Accept that resisting your normal routine is a behavior and mindset change that you have the power to accomplish. What rules and boundaries do you need to create for yourself? What values do you want and need to honor? Decisions will need to be made around these questions so that you know what you are resisting. Once you decide what it is that you are resisting, then you will want to create a way to resist, like:

- Designing a particular action to take when faced with your obstacle, like stepping away from your desk,

walking outside, and doing some mindfulness breathing.
- Creating a visual reminder of your goal—something metaphorical to focus on so you can push through the temptation to fall back into a certain habit.
- Speaking a meaningful scripture, quote, or belief every time a toxic thought arises.

Death and life are in the power of the tongue, so speak life into your resistance, and speak life to what you want your life to be.

One morning, I was sitting in the study having some devotional time, and this thought came to my head:

As you go through the day, remember *It Came To Pass.*

This is such a simple truth, and it is a reality. It doesn't matter what is going on or what you are experiencing; time will continue to move on. When you are having a rough day and being tossed about by the waves, this is a thought to cling to, so put it on a card somewhere in front of you as a reminder.

Continue focusing on the categories you explored in Step 1 and answer these three questions:

1. What new words, phrases, or sayings do I want to speak?
2. What new rules or boundaries do I choose to create?
3. What visual reminder can I create to help me focus?

Step 3: Revive

The focus for Step 3 is to revive the authentic you as you work through releasing and resisting. One way to look at this process is to fight your old behaviors as if they were cancer.

When you are going through chemotherapy and radiation, it's painful and nauseating. You have thoughts like "Is this worth it? I feel like I am dying." However, when cancer cells are dying, your body makes room to generate new healthy cells. Your hair is likely to fall out and then grow back. The chaff is burnt, and new growth appears. When I talk about reviving, I am talking about waking up to the original ideals, values, and purest beliefs you had before all of these crazy obstacles got in the way.

Answer these three questions:

1. What will I do to take care of myself on the tough days?
2. Where can I allow myself a recess, or a respite from my plan, without becoming derailed?
3. What can I do ahead of time to prepare for strategy challenges?

Step 4: Restore

Restoring yourself to a physically, emotionally, spiritually, and mentally healthy state is the goal. You have been there at some point in your life. Maybe it was last year, or when you were a child. When was that time for you, where you felt balanced, and the world was wonderful?

Answer these for each of the 4 Pillars:

1. What will restoration look like for me in each of the pillars?
2. When will I know that I am restored in each pillar?
3. What will I have done to get there?

A Tangible Strategy Action Example: Angie's 4 Pillars Detoxification Diet

When you work through your 4-step strategy, you will want to prioritize what you do, when you do it, and how you do it. It's critical to create tangible actions that can be measurable. You can choose anything on your list to work on.

As part of my plan, I chose to focus on the four personal pillars and my emotional eating.

One of the most impactful actions I can take is to put myself on a toxic releasing restrictive diet. It accomplishes a few goals for me:

- Helps me bring my body into subjection and I feel in control of myself
- Increases my energy level and mental positivity
- Gives me a goal to focus on where I can visually see and physically feel the difference

I didn't just say, "I think I will go on a diet." I thought through what I wanted to do, how it would happen, and what result I wanted. I also planned for potential obstacles.

It may sound strange, but eating less, and eating with restrictions is freeing and clarifying. You simply need to find the formula that works for you. For me personally, I found my niche diet. I tend to practice in time intervals of 11 days or 21 days, with a "3 step down" approach.

When I came away from my strategy session, I had already gone through a 21-day detox diet. I decided to repeat the process every three months to accomplish the goals I mentioned. Here's what it looks like:

Step 1 - 11 or 21-day interval: Depending on my stress level I will stick to this type of eating, knowing that I have a set beginning and set end.

Morning: An apple, orange, strawberries, or grapes.

Lunch: A salad that consists of lettuce and grilled chicken with up to 2 tablespoons of Caesar dressing.
Afternoon: Fruit again.

Dinner: Either the salad and grilled chicken like I had at lunch, or chicken or beef along with a green vegetable like green beans or broccoli.

I used to obsess over measurement, but I stopped all that and just made a reasonable judgment on the amount. If I am feeling hungry in between that, I will eat kosher dill pickles.
As far as drinks are concerned, I stick to water, coffee, and tea as much as I want. If I need sweetener, I use Truvia or Stevia. I do not allow myself to drink alcohol during this time. If I wake up feeling weak, I will have a half cup of milk.

Step 2 - Post-11 or 21-day interval: I switch to a high-protein, low-carb diet for about 2 to 3 weeks. This means I eat three meals a day with a snack in between.

Morning:	Eggs, turkey sausage, and coffee/water.
Morning Snack:	Atkins bar or high protein bar.
Lunch:	Meat plus any vegetable, and a salad or cottage cheese.

Afternoon Snack:	Beef or turkey jerky, Adkins bar, or boiled eggs (pick one).
Dinner:	Meat, vegetable, and one carb like pasta or potato.
Beverages:	I still stick with water, coffee, tea, and stevia sweetened lemonade. If I believe I am strong enough to discipline myself, I will allow an occasional glass of wine 1-2 times per week. If I am tempted to have two glasses in one day, I will cut myself off for the rest of the week.

Step 3 - Carb Integration: This is the time that I start integrating back in carbs, but I have to watch the portion sizes. I continue doing the Step 2 diet, but I might integrate a primary pasta dish in place of the meat and vegetable meal.

It's important to gauge how I am feeling. If I start feeling sluggish and tired, I pull back on portion sizes. I usually wait a couple of weeks before I try something like a cookie or piece of pie. I love pecan pie, so if I see it, I want it. I don't beat myself up if I eat it, I simply prepare for its impact. I may try to make up for it at the gym or go for a walk to work it out of my system faster.

I also keep in my mind that I will eventually revisit Step 1 to keep a toxic release cycle going.

A Word on Diet Research

A new study in 2016 from the University of California shows that you can do a Fast-Mimicking Diet in intervals of 5-days a month for three successive months and create anti-aging effects like reduction of body mass, lowering of glucose, triglycerides, and cholesterol.

Another long-term and in-depth study by Washington University in St. Louis, and the Pennington Biomedical Research Center has shown that by cutting caloric intake by 25% will dramatically reduce the chance for common diseases related to your major organs to develop, and even reduce tumor and cancer formulation. Two major outcomes have turned up for a healthier body in which anti-aging has kicked in, as well as a much more vigorous energy level.

If you want to learn more about this interesting study, visit http://www.nytimes.com/2009/10/11/magazine/11Calories-t.html

I have tried all kinds of fad diets that ended in failure. In most cases, it was my lack of discipline that did me in. When I was younger and in my early 30's, I did manage to be on track for a few years with high-protein/low-carb diets, but then my body changed and stopped responding. Then I had another child at 40, and it all fell apart after that.

I learned about my behavioral eating patterns in recent years, what was behind them, and how to counteract them. I compared my learning to what others go through as well. Here are the five patterns that have emerged:

1. We typically eat based on how we feel.
2. If we aren't feeling good, we tend to eat more sugar and carbs.
3. When we are feeling really good (in celebration mode), our diet defenses go down, and we are more likely to eat more sugar, carbs, and consume more calories in general.
4. In times of high stress, we eat more, drink more alcohol, and feel more sluggish.
5. When we feel helpless or depressed, we tend to eat as a way to control *something,* and we choose food.

Do you recognize yourself in these five patterns? Take time to examine your behavior.

- What do your eating habits look like?
- What are the results of those habits?
- How do you feel after you eat?
- Have you tried to curb them or diet?
- What was the result?
- What is the biggest trigger for you that cause loss of control regarding your eating habits?

Diet and Your Emotions

I want to emphasize that your eating habits are tied to emotions. This is the single most important point to understand. If you don't deal with your emotions and triggers, you will not succeed in improving your eating patterns. Changing an action doesn't necessarily yield different or lasting results. Rather, it is changing the experiences and beliefs you are having. This is getting to the core issue that will ultimately lead you to take actions that yield different results. Addressing your experiences and beliefs creates a different view and motivation of the situation.

For example, if you experience a stressful week, you are frustrated because you aren't getting the outcomes you expect. You are viewing this situation as impossible. At the end of the week, you believe you will feel better if you drink a case of beer. So, you decide to take action.

You head to the store, pick up the beer, and sit in your chair sucking them down. You have consumed almost 2,000 calories in one sitting, overloading your system, and your organs start to break down from the overkill. Beer has not solved your frustration; it has temporarily masked it and actually compounded your problem. The next day you wake up with the same stressful situation, a hangover, and a body that is left trying to recover from the damage it incurred.

If you want to compose your soul, you will have to deal with your eating habits. I don't care if you are skinny, healthy looking, obese, or average, eating introduces chemicals into your body that create change and reactions. These chemicals marry up (or break up) with your existing physiological structure. Additionally, it impacts your brain and the way you process things. There is nothing you can do to bypass that fact. I can sum it up like this:

What you eat influences your emotions, cognitive processes, and behavior. When you eat more than you need to, your brain gets cloudy and overcast, and your reactions will reflect this. When you eat lots of sugar and empty calorie carbs/fats, it's like putting sugar into the gas tank of your car. The result is a stopped up engine that won't go. These habits do not solve your problems; they multiply your problems.

So what do you do? My experience is that you can simultaneously deal with your emotional triggers and your diet at the same time. Rewiring your experiences and beliefs around emotional triggers is a primary goal. From a diet standpoint, it's a supporting objective. I've found that when you are restricting your diet, you are less reactive and emotional. In fact, you have a nice layer of calm when you are in the proper dieting zone.

Think of it like an army of troops living inside you. Your inner troops are fighting all kinds of battles. When you are in the right diet zone, your body has more of the resources available to fight off stress. When you are not in a good diet zone, you have to split up those troops so they can try to process the baggage of toxins that excessive and unhealthy foods bring. You've created a civil war inside your body, and you won't have enough troops to meet the stress battle.

Exercise: A Metaphorical Way to Look at Your Eating Habits

You may be challenged with accepting the word, "restrictive." We love freedom, and we don't like someone putting limits on us, right? Let me be clear; I am not advocating starvation or anorexia. That behavior is toxic and unhealthy. I am promoting the regulation of your food intake.

Shift your perspective of the word, "restrictive," to a positive, structured, and safe word. Think of it in terms of keeping bad things out that seek to harm you. You are not restricting yourself; you are restricting the external dangers and enemies while maintaining a fortress around your beautiful castle.

Imagine that you are that castle.

What is knocking at your gate? You know that to survive, you have to let down the drawbridge and let things in from time to time. You do need food, and it is outside the gate, but you choose what comes in. You do this from an operational safety standpoint. You decide what comes in, and what is not safe. You choose the quality items, not the substandard quantity things.

There may be times when you choose to let a cookie in the door. Is it wrong? Well, nobody is going to berate you for letting it in, but you have to be prepared for the consequences of that and managing the "visit."

Macadamia nut cookies have their other cookie friends who are lonely. Once they get inside, they want to convince you to that should invite their other friends in.

You find yourself lowering the drawbridge. Before you know it, they have come in and made residence inside your fat cells and are taking up space causing your "staff" to wait on them hand and foot. The staff becomes exhausted from making them comfortable, and the civil war starts. Hopefully, you get the point. It is your decision.

Take time to reflect on these questions:

- When you lower your drawbridge, what are you typically letting in?
- What is this "visitor's" calling card?
- When does this visitor usually show up?
- What emotion is tugged?
- What experience and belief do you need to change to turn away this visitor?

Lock It In

The 4-Step Strategy is a change. It's uncomfortable. You might try to kick start a plan, but it falls flat. This happens to me from time to time. The secret is to not give up after the first try.

Kick-start until you can lock it in.

Can you think of a time you decided to make a change, and you struggled to stick with it? You knew the change was important, you wanted to do it, and there was even a sense of judgment around it. Since we are on the topic of food and diet, let's say you knew you needed to drop those 15 pounds, and you shouldn't eat that hot fudge brownie sundae at Applebee's, but it was Grandma's birthday, and you knew she would be offended that you didn't partake in the festivities. You ended up eating that luscious dessert, blowing your diet. You haven't quite locked it in because you wanted to be harmonious with Grandma.

Then, something happened to create urgency within you. For example, you saw a video of yourself and seeing your size shocked you. A few neurotransmitters kicked in due to your emotional panic, and you suddenly became resolved to lose the fat. You developed a "do or die" way of thinking. You got a revelation, and suddenly you were able to get on track. You found yourself speaking in a definitive *yes* or *no*.

Locking it in would have resulted in you saying no to the dessert no matter how everyone responded. Your value of being healthy and fit was important to honor, and your mind was fixed because you knew you were standing for something critical to you.

Switch to a different scenario. You are working at an office where a certain coworker keeps cutting you off when you talk, and you tell yourself that you aren't going to put up with it anymore because it leaves you feeling disrespected and minimized. Yet, to date, you have not confronted that person about his behavior.

Instead, you talk to everyone but that person, and everyone agrees that it's not right to be treated that way. You find yourself in a cycle of resentment and building anger but repressed. This is not overcoming. It is your undoing.

Then one day, your coworker goes too far and insults your kid in the process of cutting you off. This changes the game, and you lock it in by confronting the coworker about the impact his behavior. The value you have around protecting your child has created urgency, and you are finally resolved to deal with the insulter.

Think about the decision around selling your house. Compare your daily actions when you are just living in the house, and it isn't for sale. You could be thinking about it, but you've not fully committed. It impacts how you approach the cleanliness and readiness of your home. You are more likely not to make your bed, run the dishwasher as often, or pick up as frequently. Now switch to the fact that you have decided to put it up for sale, contacted the agent, and now you have a sign in the front yard. People are going to be coming through your house.

Your mindset changes. You suddenly become a drill sergeant demanding an orderly house, and your whole routine changes to accommodate potential buyers. You go from a *maybe to* a *must* way of thinking. There's no question, you must have all laundry put away, you must power wash the outside, and you must clean out the garage. You lock it in, and your direction changes.

What causes you to go through this transition?

You now have a valid and life altering reason to change, not just because you should do it or it would be nice. Locking it in is driven by what you value as important, and an emotional trigger has been activated.

You are valuing one thing over the other. You may choose not to confront your coworker because you value harmony (or have a fear of conflict) over everything else. What you may not realize is that you could be fighting against that harmony value when you don't confront the bully coworker.

There are multiple ways you can get tripped up, but once you lock it in by getting the sense of urgency, you are on a path. Nobody is going to get in your way.

EXERCISE: Planning for the Obstacle of Your Family

Your castle security can easily be threatened by the people you love the most. In the spirit of celebration or with the desire to comfort you, they show up at your castle offering you food and drinks that you don't need. They also offer other distractions, like complaining when you don't have supper on the table right at 5:30 or taking your time for granted. Remember that *you* are the decision maker and you have the power to refuse in order to honor your process.

My mother and I were recently talking about diet and its effects on the people around us. She is an avid dieter with many years of experience, and I cherish her wisdom and insights on this topic.

I was on day 12 of a 21-day restrictive diet cycle and feeling exceptionally well. My mind was finally getting back to a place of clarity and sharpness, my body was in subjection, and I just felt so much happier. I had managed to drastically reduce my reactivity to tough situations because of my clean eating. The result was that I was feeling more confident and in control of my circumstances.

In spite of this personal satisfaction, I noticed that my dieting made others uncomfortable. How did I know? Because they told me and showed me.

On the first day of my diet, my husband bought me a bottle of wine and offered me a glass. In the following few days, he started making comments about my diet. One night he picked up Kentucky Fried Chicken and seemed perturbed that I chose to stick to my salad.

We went to dinner one evening, and he ordered two full appetizers for three people, encouraging me to eat them. I was in my office working when he came in and said I just had to watch this video of a 3-pound cinnamon roll being made, and asked, "Who would eat something like that?!?!" Even my mother jumped on the bandwagon one day, trying to encourage me to eat some french fries. "Oh, this won't hurt you to cheat a little bit!"

This may not seem like a big deal, but my husband doesn't normally buy or pour me a glass of wine unless I ask him to. I usually get my own wine and pour my own glass. He never comments when I overeat or eat ridiculous, unhealthy foods. He never runs out to Dunkin' Donuts and gets my favorite kind until he knows I am trying to stay on track with my diet.

My mother smiled and said, "Dieting is threatening to other people. It reminds them of what they aren't doing or controlling in their lives. They feel guilty. Like me. Sometimes people get insecure because you are in control of yourself. Some spouses may feel threatened because you are getting thin and are possibly becoming more attractive to others." Even more attractive than you already are.

For my husband, I know that his love language is centered around food. So, I realize that if I am limiting my food, he is interpreting that as limiting love, and he personalizes that. I don't think he would ever admit to that, but he lets me know in different ways.

The bottom line is that you have to be aware of the impacts of your choice and be prepared to protect your castle. Don't quit taking care of yourself because someone else might get upset about it. Instead, be prepared to reassure people that you still love them and care about them. Be cognizant of others' insecurities and challenges, so you can keep yourself from failing because of their insecurities.

Reflection Questions:

- What pushback do you anticipate when you activate your strategy?
- What Inner Critics will you need to shut down?
- What Inner Committee Member will you call forth to support your goals?
- What can you do to nip others' insecurities in the bud?

CHAPTER 14

DEALING WITH DIFFICULT
PEOPLE AND BULLIES

"Psychologists will tell you to run from a bully. That advice is contrary to my Code of Courage."
-Angie Nuttle

Imagine that you have reached your goals toward composing your soul.

You have figured out your natural algorithm. You understand how your pre-existing conditions tend to filter your perceptions, and you know how your brain is wired. You have your inner committee humming with joy, and your inner critics are easy to shut down. You've implemented a strategy around your 4 Personal Pillars, and you feel great.

Finally, you have gotten some clarity around your existing and meaning. You know why you exist, what you need to do, and you are ready to rock the world. You are positioning yourself to step into your mission and the role you are being called to do (whatever that may be).

And then you realize that you have to deal with difficult people.

We've talked about a few challenging situations already. In most cases, the work starts with you managing yourself. Generally, you can resolve issues through aligning with your natural algorithm, enforcing your boundaries, and good old-fashioned conversation. However, we need to talk about a different breed of people who don't care about you or your boundaries.

Bullying has skyrocketed in our society, and it is alarming. You've probably encountered a bully in some capacity, known one, or have personally felt the stun-gun of one. Two words:

1. Painful.
2. Ignominious (public humiliation, shaming, and discrediting).

Experiencing the wrath of bullies is like an electric shock to the system because your innermost point of vulnerability is infiltrated. No one wants to be publicly humiliated, minimized, or trashed, and that's exactly what bullies do to people. It's part of their defense mechanism to manage their insecurities and fears at the expense of others.

It's sad when you think about it. When a person is so embittered, and out of touch with others, it has to be a very lonely place. You know they have experienced something detrimental in their history, and it can be any number of negative experiences ranging from a basic lack of love to severe abuse.

And bullies start young.

STORY: Nightmare on Woodfield Drive

The summer of 2016 is one I will always remember, not because of a great vacation or joyous occasion, but because of the bully.

Mackenzie started the summer off with her usual perky quest to book the calendar with friend sleepovers and creative adventures. At 8-years-old, she was on top of the world and loving life.

Within the first few weeks, she went into entrepreneur mode and concocted a cupcake bakery, a nail salon, and a dog walking business. Her passion was fueled each time one of her neighborhood friends partook in her business experiments with her. The result would be incessant laughing and of course, a sleepover.

As June rounded the corner, Kenzie befriended a girl down the street who was a year older (we will call her Darcy). I thought it was odd that this girl had lived nearby and Kenzie had never mentioned her, until now.

The relationship bloomed fast, and the two girls were inseparable, along with the girl's younger sister, who was always present and always quiet. They bounced back and forth between houses, constant texting and Facetiming when they were apart, and eventually, the sleepovers began. The girls were inseparable.

Then, the relationship went dark. Here's my recollection:

"Mom, I am not feeling good about something."

"What's going on, babe?"

"Darcy keeps sending me mean texts, and I don't like them."

I pause for a moment. Sounds like a job for Executive Coach with a twist of mom wisdom.

"Hmmm. Sounds like you need to politely let Darcy know you need some space, and you don't feel like talking right now. I like your plan of spending time with some of your other friends. "

She seems to accept that advice. Problem solved.

Kenzie has always been a free spirit. She tells me that she misses hanging out with some of her other neighborhood friends. She's excited because some of them are coming back from their summer vacations. She is ready to venture back to play with them today, and Operation Reconnect is activated.

A week or so later, I notice that Mackenzie is showing up as negative, self-defeating, and with unusually raw emotion at home. We go to cheerleading practice that evening, and in the middle of it all, she has a breakdown.

"I can't do it! I can't do it!"

I'm flabbergasted. What is happening that my baby girl is falling apart like this? Thoughts run through my head. Is the pressure of cheerleading too much? Is something happening to her mental state? Do I need to take her to a psychologist? I don't understand!

She is sobbing incoherently as I try to talk to her. Executive Coach tells me to just be with her, comfort her, and soothe her until she can return to a calm place. In the meantime, I am processing all of this so I can resolve Mackenzie's pain.

She is falling apart for some reason. Her whole demeanor has changed from bright and shiny to sad and pessimistic. I am alarmed at her sudden shift in outlook and her lack of motivation. My husband and I investigate the best available source of information: Mackenzie's iPad.

Looking at the data on Kenzie's iPad, we discover that my advice to Mackenzie has backfired. Not only has the communication continued after Mackenzie proclaimed her need for space, Darcy's texts and calls have intensified to outright harassment with 15 FaceTime calls in 15 minutes. What is more disturbing is that Darcy has recruited another girl, Sonya, who has been texting Mackenzie repeatedly with harassing messages and threats on a minute-by-minute basis.

When I see the venomous texts and infinite number of calls, I wake up fast. This isn't some passing phase. Although I am extremely proud of my daughter's level of maturity in her responses, this is a real, live bully situation, and it has to stop.

My husband sends a message to Darcy that Mackenzie would not be communicating with her anymore, and he deletes all of the threatening messages. He also blocks Darcy and Sonya from being able to contact our daughter. We are done with all of this "being nice stuff."

Over the next several days, we work on a recovery process with Kenzie and even take a trip to Kings Island to get our kid back somehow. What helps her the most is to talk through the experience, and understanding why Darcy has behaved the way she did. I want her to understand that Darcy's actions had nothing to do with her.

My daughter knows that I work with leaders, so I give her the 7 Truths about Bullies and a few critical leadership lessons from this experience:

#1-Bullying is a learned behavior and a coping mechanism for people who are fearful.

#2-Bullies are bullies because they are insecure about themselves and need to dominate others to feel secure.

#3-Bullies recruit weak and fearful people (who eventually become cronies) to support their bullying work, and they condition their cronies through bullying.

#4-Those "close" to bullies have learned to be quiet, so they don't get injured.

#5-Bully kids grow up to be bully adults and are difficult, if not impossible, to change.

#6-Bully adults tend to bully their way into positions of power.

#7-Bullies are not leaders. They are bullies (and wrecking balls).

We have to take the learnings in bits and pieces over the rest of the summer. When fall comes, it's time to head back to school and leave as much of the experience behind her.

On the first day of 3rd grade, we are standing at the bus stop in anticipation. I see a bit of that glimmery, bright shine in my little girl as I video her prancing around with her book bag full of school goodies.

"I hope I find a new friend today!" She proclaims it with enthusiasm.

My heart smiles. She is slowly coming back to herself, although she is carrying a scar. She is still a little skeptical, and not quite 100% yet.

A few weeks later, I look into her backpack, and I find the book, *How Full Is Your Bucket*? My heart yells in triumph! The kid is showing me she is on the road to recovery, and her goal now is to encourage others through her harrowing experience. A few more percentage points for Mackenzie! She's getting to 100%, and working her way up. She shares one day that a new girl has come to school, and she sits with her at lunch because nobody else offered.

"She was lonely and scared, and I wanted to help her."

100%.

What Happens When Bully Kids Grow up

Kid bullies grow up to be adult bullies. You can only go so far to block them on your phone. When you get into the workplace, it's hard to get away from them because they are lurking everywhere.

The bully may be someone you report to, which is a challenging place to be in. What is frustrating is that bullies do push their way into leadership positions. Sometimes it feels like everyone is turning a blind eye to these difficult people, and the cost is high.

People become less productive and even leave their jobs to avoid the bullying experience. When individual business people are impacted, so are the organizations they work for. Unfortunately, most organizations tend to rationalize the behavior:

"Well, he's not great with people, but he IS getting results."

"Maybe over time she will calm down when she sees our progress."

"If we promote this bully, we hope he will be nicer and more productive."

These are lies organizations tell themselves to avoid the conflict. The truth is that a single bully getting results is causing 100 other people to be six times less effective in their performance.

Bullies don't suddenly decide to change. They feed off of fear, lack of action, and lack of accountability. Organizations who allow bullies to remain in leadership positions pay a hefty price for their lack of ownership of the problem.

What Research Says about the Cost of Bullies

According to the Workplace Bullying Institute, you can calculate the bully's impact on the bottom line with this equation:

Lack of engagement + Opportunity Lost + Absenteeism + Presenteeism + Legal Defense Cost + Dispute Resolution + Trial Costs + Settlements + WC/Disability Fraud Investigation = The Routine Cost of Allowing Bullies to Harm Others with Impunity.

Harrison Psychological Associates reports the business costs of bullying to employers where people are being harassed, within a two-year period, is more than $180 million in lost time and productivity.

Gary Namie's study at The Workplace Bullying & Trauma Institute (WBTI), (2003 n=1,000) shows 70% of people bullied (targets) leave their current position of employment after working with the employer for an average of 6.7 years. According to Namie's study, a target endures the bullying for an average of 23 months before they leave the aggressive environment.

STORY: THE CEO Bully

I was contracted by a well-known sports organization to assess, construct, and implement a new human resources structure for them at the recommendation of their advisory board. It was a surprise to me that this organization didn't have any HR structure in place, but I was excited to have the opportunity, so my team and I jumped right in.

I met with the CEO and a small team who would be partnering with us throughout the project and instantly recognized why the organization was so far behind. I quickly assessed that the CEO was a classic bully. He controlled every action, every decision, and every word spoken by his staff in the meetings.

He established his parameters up front, stating that he would not be doing what we told him and he was only here to appease the board. He also noted that no part of the work would include soliciting feedback or talking to any of the staff, nor creating any processes that invited 360 feedback.

The team, afraid of his emotional outbursts, was conditioned to adjust based on his responses and actions. When he reacted with manic positivity, the team members laughed and lightened up along with him. When he was on the hunt for a victim, everyone cowered down in hopes of avoiding his wrath. Members of the team came to us privately to voice their fears but never voiced them outside of our conversations. They were mortified and petrified.

My consulting team, on the other hand, challenged the CEO to ensure that the organization was in compliance with employment law. It was a huge part of our contract, and we were legally bound to perform to its stipulations.

It was a difficult experience, to say the least. I used my best relationship and coaching skills to manage the situation. We were astounded throughout the project, watching him writhe back and forth out of control like a riding bull stuck in his pen.

He made concerted efforts to get us to drop the project, making derogatory comments about my lead consultant, who was female and pregnant. We had to have a few conversations to stay the course. I knew this guy was trying to shake us so he could present it as a failed idea to his board. I was much more determined than he to hang on and weather the tsunami waves he was causing.

The project finally came to a completion. In our last meeting, we recommended a permanent HR person to be put in place to maintain and build upon the structure we created. It was one of the most incredible meetings I've ever been in but in a horrific way.

As we made our recommendations, we watched this grown man move into a well-orchestrated melt down in front of the project team. He felt out of control, so he yelled, cried crocodile tears, then stomped out of the meeting, rambling incoherently about how he had to make a public statement to news media about a controversial situation happening with the organization. That was the last time I saw him, and the last memory I have of him. A perfectly distracting exit for someone who was unable to dominate the outcome.

Shortly after the meeting and project completion, we were informed that the CEO made a choice to bring someone onboard to fill the HR position (and who incidentally had no HR background, period). We had a briefing meeting to gladly transition everything over, and cut ties.

Several months later, the organization and its CEO were back in the news media due to that controversial situation. Shortly after the hype, a news report came out, and the CEO had "resigned." I suspect that his board helped him to make that decision only after it had cost their reputation. Either way, I know the people who were working there had to be completely relieved. Years and years of oppression ended in one day.

How Should a Bully Be approached?

Many psychologists will tell you *not to* confront a bully. I don't fully agree with that in terms of *avoiding* a bully. People need to understand how they impact you, and you need to express yourself to work those toxic experiences out of your body and your mind so you can live with yourself. I've learned a lot of bullies out there don't even realize how they are showing up. Others know it and use it as their way of gaining control and power.

Bullies dismantle a person's emotional balance. As a coach who deals with bully victims, I've seen people suffer at the hands of bullies in ways that left them professionally crippled. Anguished over the deep humiliation, changing their lives dramatically.

If you are in an executive position and you are aware of a bully situation, address it. That person needs to be held accountable and the longer you leave that person in a leadership position, the more damage it causes to your people, culture, and your business results. Bullies help put businesses into bankruptcy. In my human resources experience, 80% of people leave the company because of a bad leader and/or a bully.

If you are in a subordinate position to a bully, I encourage you to focus on the situation, not the person. Bullying is like a disease that needs treatment. I'll expand on this more in the next chapter.

How to Deal with Organizational Bullies and Other Wrecking Balls

Before you decide to deal with bullies and others who are equally difficult, you will want to think through what your general position is going to be. I stress that awareness is a key step in overcoming the situation. Understanding why bullies do what they do is helpful, but it doesn't excuse their behavior, and it certainly doesn't make you feel any better.

You have four choices when it comes to a bully situation: Diplomacy, War, Holding your position, or Rethinking your strategy (or retreating).

Diplomacy is only a short-term solution for dealing with bullies because they rarely honor boundaries and disregard prior agreements. Most of us end up retreating or trying to rethink our strategies.

Holding your position is a viable option if you want to continue in your present state and stand your ground. In my situation with the sports organization CEO, I chose the tactic of holding my position. The project was short-term, and I didn't have enough energy to go to war, which would have meant circumventing his authority and going straight to his board. I was also early in start-up phase for my company, and I didn't want a potential political storm to put my team's jobs at risk.

In all transparency, I took it to God and asked Him to take that burden and deal with it in how He saw fit. He did a great job although it took several months to see the answer.

When is the right time for war?

I want to talk about this particular strategy because most of us tend to run from it. War is like a hero moment. There comes a day when you forsake all political correctness to stand for something greater. There's no more collaboration, no more silence, or meekly defending yourself. The circumstances are palpable and even dire.

You are facing a now or never moment. It could be that:

- You must speak now or forever hold your peace (the door of opportunity is closing).
- You must defend a treasured value, idea, or principle (instead of allowing your beliefs to be stepped on).
- You must rise from an oppressive circumstance (Rocky).
- You must protect a sacred right (Martin Luther).
- You must stand for the life of someone or something (Mother Teresa).
- You must do something, or lose your dignity, self-respect, and self-worth (along with everyone else's respect).

Ask yourself: Am I ready to go to war with this bully? What will you stand for and what will you protect?

If one of the bullet points above strikes a chord with you, then the answer may be yes.

The Things You Need to Know Before Going to War

First and foremost, bullies want to isolate their victims. I've been around enough bullies to know that they are afraid to operate alone. They force others to validate them by demanding they turn against or attack the victim. Bullies also like to separate their victims from the rest of the group so he or she can't gather strength. For both the bully and the victim, there is power in numbers.

Secondly, your soul must be composed and centered for you to take things to the battlefield. If you are confident that you are living in alignment with your values and you are your authentic self, it's a good start. Know that the bully will look for your vulnerable spot and take a big nasty swing at it.

I hear those of you who are more gentle and sympathetic saying, "But that bully is a person who has been hurt." I agree and understand that, but unless you are a trained psychologist that the bully has sought for help, your best bet is to let the professionals sort out his or her behavior.

My position is that it's a God job.

Strategies for Going to War

Here are a few strategies I recommend you use to deal with bullies in leadership positions:

1. **When dealing with a bully, start with assessing yourself first.**

Before you try to conquer Goliath, get clear on why you are reacting the way that you are. People who are more severely affected by bullies are:

- Predisposed to having a fearful nature and worrying about situations such as change, fitting in, and perfectionism.
- Opposed to conflict and have a strong need for harmony.
- Dealing with (or have dealt with) one or more traumatizing experiences in their personal lives.
- Afflicted with a low self-esteem and self-worth issues.
- Holding on to a belief that they can befriend and change a bully—and suffer disappointment when that doesn't happen.

2. When choosing to take action, weigh your strategic options.

Think through the following options with your eyes wide open, knowing that you can't change that other person; you can only change yourself and manage the situation. All of the four strategies I mentioned require strong mental and emotional fortitude to be activated.

- *Is this the time to be Diplomatic?* I don't mean letting someone walk all over you. I mean calmly treating the bully just like you would any other person, with respect, dignity, and a listening ear. Especially if it is in a group setting. Have the guts to connect later with the bully in a one-on-one situation and give him or her feedback to clear your conscience.

- *Should You Hold Your Position?* Are you being questioned about something that you are an expert in or have solid knowledge about, or are your values being challenged? As much as you want to jump into victim mode, or jump across the table and throat punch the bully, don't. Politely, but firmly stand your ground using neutral, objective language. Clearly and calmly state your position with your reason and don't backtrack. A bully can smell a lack of confidence a mile away and will exploit it, so show up with executive presence.

- *Is it time to rethink your approach and strategy?* Are you going down the same rabbit hole you have before in meetings with this person? Stop and just hold your silence— temporarily. It's better to be quiet than to jump into a trap. Get to a safety zone and rethink how you need to respond differently to that situation.

> Careful though, you could overuse this strategy and succumb to victim mode.

- *Is it time for war?* You've done everything you can on your own, and now it is time to gather the troops. Remember, bullies have a hard time standing up against a group—there is power in numbers. Talk to others who feel the same way and collectively approach your senior leadership. I've also seen where the group has requested a meeting with the bully to give feedback successfully.

3. Start a Bully Prevention Program at Work.

This sounds like grade school, and it's similar in concept. Proactively starting an advocacy group is a new trend on the business horizon. In the business setting, you might call this the Social and Leadership Responsibility Program or some other acronym type name like NO-BULL-E (you are welcome to use that one for free).

4. Recognize that you have four ultimatums.

It always comes down to doing what you can live with.

1. *Do nothing and keep getting bullied.*
2. *Change yourself and your reaction.*
3. *Confront the situation at a higher or different level.*
4. *Leave.*

Each choice has its consequences, but I encourage you to suffer through the blows and stand up to the situation. People will thank you for having the courage to do what they don't want to do. I've personally learned that running doesn't work. You will run from one bully right into another one, and your resilience will wear off.

Bottom line, business people have to stand up for what is right, and it takes boldness.

The next time you face a bully, ask yourself if you should give control to that person, or if you should be true to your values—no matter the cost. When you choose to let the bully come in and control you emotionally, it's not just about you. You are setting a precedent that it is okay to be bullied. Think about your audience: Your organization, your family, and the generation to come after you.

Tools to Use on The Stinky Fish

If you read my first book, *From Invisible to Incredible: The Secret to Brilliant Executive Presence,* then you know something about auto responders. If you've attended my boot camps or Mastermind Program, you have also learned about deflecting people who are out to step on others to make themselves feel better.

Nothing can throw you off balance like a person who wants to assassinate your character, or who needs to intimidate someone to validate their own existence. When you encounter this person over and over, it's time to *flay the fish.*

Fish stink. You know a fish is nearby because you smell it. You may not see it immediately. If it is in front of you, you know it is there, but the smell is coming from the inside. To pinpoint the origin of the smell, you have to cut that fish wide open. You have to *flay* it.

The same principle applies when you are dealing with a difficult person or a bully. Many times that person asks a question with the sole purpose of tripping you up. Many of us have fallen into the trap of being stun-gunned by their questions or being skillfully led into a hole that leaves us looking incompetent, and the bully reveling in self-aggrandizing victory.

How do you flay this fish? In communication terms, you have to get to the heart of the matter.

Let's say that you are presenting a proposal in front of a team of leaders, and you want them to commit budget to the project. You know that Bob is a bully and he throws a question at you like, "And what will we do when we run out of money on this project and have to take a loan to cover the rest of the cost?"

This situation is a stinky fish. It's easy to stare at this stinky fish and wonder, "What is the purpose of this? I must defend my position." We are likely to just play with the stinky fish with long explanations, fumbling around and eventually looking uneducated, but instead, you recognize that the fish has to be flayed. You've got to open it up, let the gasses out, and clear the air.

Flaying might look something like this:

"Interesting question, Bob. What is your concern behind that question and what can I do to help alleviate your fear?"

Or this: "Bob, what I hear you saying is that you are fearful that something may go wrong. Talk to me about your concern."

You've just flayed it wide open to get to the real issue surrounding the question: Bob's fear.

It doesn't solve the problem yet, but it takes the conversation to a transparent level on overcoming the emotion and looking at real solutions. People in business do this every day. It's also a chance for you to put the squash effect to Bob's attempt to assassinate you, and influence the room with a statement like: "There are very intelligent people in this room. There is power in numbers, so I know that with all of us pulling in the same direction, we can manage the budget and prevent a disastrous outcome. I know you are a person who appreciates those kinds of results."

Tool: Learn to Use Auto responders

What if you aren't that quick on your feet to think of an intelligent response? You rely on *auto responders*. I alluded to these a few paragraphs back. These are pre-planned statements that give you a chance to overcome the stun-gun of a bully. An auto responder might look like this:

"Thank you for that question. I would like to give that some thought and come back to you with an intelligent response by tomorrow."

Or, "I appreciate your question. Tell me more about what you are thinking so I can put some thought into it."

An auto responder is a conversation structure or a template that you can use when you know you have a stinky fish, but you aren't able to flay it at the moment. It consists of three things:

1. A verbal demonstration of appreciation or thankfulness to the person who is speaking to you.
2. A pause or delay statement that allows you to get back on your feet.
3. If warranted, a commitment to respond and work with the person, even if it is at a later time.

Auto responders give you a sense of comfort and structure, so you don't go completely off the rails when faced with a bully.

When a bully attacks, you may be worried about how you come across, that people might question your character or even think less of you somehow. Memorize this phrase and explore its truth for yourself:

You don't have to speak about your character. Let your character speak for itself.

I promise that as long as you are operating with full authenticity, confidence, and integrity, people see it. You may not feel like it at the moment, but people are outside of the situation, watching the bully, and thinking, "That bully is a wrecking ball!" You make a mistake only when you spar sarcastically with that bully, or you revert to *scared customer service representative mode,* "Yes sir, I will jump through those hoops right away." "Yes ma'am, I will do whatever you say!" You are the adult, so let someone else play the Parent or Child modes.

One more thing.

You deserve to be in the room. You are not less than. You belong at the table. Your worth is not based on what someone refuses to see.

CHAPTER 15

GET YOUR MISSION ON

"Your mission is not a place you go to; it's something you bring to every place you go." -Angie Nuttle

Saint George Island, Florida, was made for me.

The small barrier island off the panhandle gulf coast is often touted as the *forgotten coast*. My appreciation for its nickname is enhanced by the fact that I can go there and forget about my worries while enjoying the uncrowded beaches.

It's the one place in this world where I can go and fully decompress and regain my composure.

As my family and I travel the 4-mile bridge that connects the mainland to the island, I feel myself transition from Madam CEO to Fully Present, a woman who is balancing all of her personal pillars. The daily challenges of being a business owner are left behind. I can feel comfortable about having my out-of-office email notification and turn off my responsiveness. I can shift to what other people might call a normal life where my focus is on the family, fun, and recovery.

I would like to think that I could retire there one day. I could buy a beach house and sit on the shore watching the waves come every morning. As I soak in the mornings with my coffee, I imagine that I can feel the years of stress, both good and bad, shed from my body and blow away with the sea winds. My feet are buried in the sand, and I can feel the salty air soaking into my skin as I sit in my rustic lounge chair.

But I know myself well.

As much as I love this place with my whole heart, I know it is not a permanent answer to a composed soul. Saint George Island is my place of respite, safety, and tranquility.

I could probably do the same de-stressing routine for a couple of weeks before I start thinking, "Okay, what do I do now?" By the end of 30 days, I would probably create a new strategy for a new business and start working on it immediately.

Just as I sat at Christian Park School that sunny day, loving life in that moment of freedom, something calls me back to face the world, and I am compelled to continue moving. I'm reminded that I still have a whole life waiting for me to show up to.

My natural algorithm won't let me just sit, fade away into the sunset, and die. I was born to be productive, and connect with other people to encourage them. There are people out there who are stuck in emotional prisons, and they need the keys to get out. Others are wandering around in the wilderness of work trying to survive, sacrifice, and prove themselves. They are looking for a guide to get them focused. Many more are in crisis and need someone who's been there to talk them through it.

I am not designed to sit around and do nothing. Neither are you.

You are here for a mission. You are being called to come up higher. What is it that you are here to do and be? After reading this book, you probably still have a lot of questions. And you may even wonder why I keep bringing up your mission when this book is about composing your soul.

The two are made to fit together and feed off one another.

You can attain a composed soul when you know what value you bring, and are living it out. It's not just about living your mission; it's also how you are living it. This means authentically walking the path that allows you to honor your natural algorithm.

And there are other people involved. Every single person on this planet has a target audience for his or her mission. The target may be small with a focus on one person at a time, or a very large audience with thousands or even millions of people. Either way, every person and every encounter matters.

There are so many stories I could share with you at this moment about chance encounters that have led to missions being born. One that stands out to me is the first time I met Miriam Ferguson.

STORY: Miriam the Golfer, Leader, and Seeker

There are no accidents when it comes to meeting people. Every place you go is an opportunity to live your mission.

I was speaking at a Chiropractic Leadership Conference in Colorado when one such opportunity revealed itself. Here is my recollection:

It's the morning after an incredible day of speaking and teaching. Although I am tired and suffering from a lack of oxygen, I have an underlying sense of elation about the prior day's event. I'm supposed to be out in front of the lodge at 5 a.m. for my ride to the Denver airport.

My natural algorithm is crying about it all. 5 a.m. isn't my best hour to be awake, plus I am in a time zone that is 2 hours behind my normal zone. I only get one cup of coffee in my room, which is not enough. Luggage ready, I trudge in the darkness to the front of the lodge. I'm hoping there is coffee somewhere, but the prospects are grim.

As I approach the rudimentary benches outside, another lady with a giant golf bag is there waiting. We sit there for a few minutes quietly. I figure she probably hasn't had much coffee, which is the same plight I am experiencing. I let myself off the hook in terms of striking up a conversation because no one wants to tell his or her life story at this time in the morning.

Of course, after a few minutes, she pipes up about the late timing of the airport van. We introduce ourselves and talk about why we've been at the lodge. I'm a speaker, and she's a golfer. Her name is Miriam, and she brightens up as she talks about her recent adventure with pro golfers like Nancy Lopez.

The conversation deepens, and we start talking about her career. She's an executive with a healthcare organization, and she's facing some human resources challenges that are driving her crazy. Now she is talking my language, and I share some expert advice with her. I give her my card and tell her to give me a call if she wants to catch up sometime.

A van pulls up, and it looks like our ride is here. We start loading up our bags when the driver checks for our names on his list.

"Looks like one of you is not on this van. There's another van coming in a few minutes."

He looks at me, and I've drawn the short straw. A voice enters my head and tells me to give her a copy of my first book. I obey, and Miriam expresses her appreciation of having something to read on her way back home. She gets in the van and drives off into the crack of dawn.

I don't anticipate hearing from her again, but a few weeks later, I get an email from her, and we touch base by phone shortly afterward. It's like God has brought us together from two different places, and here we are.

She asks me to be her executive coach, so we start to work together over the next several months. The gorgeous part about the whole situation is that Miriam is drawn to this question of mission in her life. She ends up enrolling in my Mastermind Program and rapidly begins to assess her mission while learning to remove inner critics and personal obstacles.

Over time, Miriam blooms, and everyone in her workplace sees it. As far as mission is concerned, she's made critical breakthroughs that will now allow her to move forward in the direction she is being called to go.

As I write this book, Miriam knows that she is called to teach in the areas of healthcare for women, leadership, and it somehow involves golf. Serendipity is kicking in, and she has been invited into the inner circle of a professional golfing association with well-known names. It's evolving right in front of her! She is preparing for this significant step with a move to Florida.

This is why every encounter matters. People need to be encouraged and guided. They also need keys, so they unlock their prison doors. Just like Miriam.

And now, she is going to live her mission and be a catalyst for someone else.

How Do You Find Your Mission?

I am always excited when I am working with clients who are on the verge of discovering what they are here for. I am even more thrilled when they see it coming over the horizon.

Recently, I was coaching a young and brilliant gentleman who was a new college graduate. He had gone out into his field of business sales and immediately realized it wasn't for him. He opted to start working for his CEO father and learn the manufacturing business, which was vastly different than his intended career path. He was out on the production floor learning the ropes as he was trying to understand the operational processes.

As we talked about his path, I asked him what he felt his mission was. He thought for a moment, contemplating if he should say it out loud. He then stated resolutely:

"I don't know exactly what my role is or how long I am supposed to be here, but I know I am supposed to be a leader. We are going through very turbulent times in this world, and I know I am being prepared to lead people out of danger and bring them to higher ground."

Now here is someone who understands the general path that he needs to follow and he just needs to go through experiences, trusting that as he looks for the right roads, this mission will mature at the right time.

Your mission has a way of finding you.

A great example of this can be found in the story of an airline flight attendant named Shelia Fedrick. Shelia noticed a girl on the plane she was servicing. The girl was disheveled and sitting with an older, well-dressed man, and it struck the flight attendant as odd.

After getting the stiff brush off by the man, Shelia left a message in the bathroom in hopes that the girl would find it.

She did. And she wrote back, "I need help."

The courageous flight attendant notified authorities, and it turns out the girl was caught in human trafficking. Thanks to Shelia's intuition and fast action, the girl was rescued.

Now Shelia has begun to discover her mission. She did not leave her job as a flight attendant and become a human trafficking expert (although it could happen). She continues to fly the friendly skies while turning on her "safety intuition radar" to all of the diverse people who may need her help as they get on her flights. Way to go Shelia!

How Do You Answer: "What Is my mission?"

There are preconceived notions that having a mission means doing something like going to Uganda to teach underprivileged kids or working at a nonprofit thrift store to support homeless people. These are literal mission fields, but not everyone can run to a foreign country and work in a soup kitchen or teach math to kids that don't speak the same language.

I surveyed a few people to understand how they were viewing the word *mission*. My question for them was this: Do you have a mission? If so, what is it?"

I got varied responses like this:

"Doesn't everyone have a mission in some aspect?! I want to be successful at my job. I mean a true asset to my company. Not Title Entitlement. I want to show myself that, with persistence, hard work and believing in myself can pay off. I want this to be instilled in my children. I want them to believe that no circumstance or "No" can break your drive! It is just another road that may need to be built first!" *Mandy M.*

"I believe my mission is to help businesses connect and stay connected to the right talent/people." *Julie L.*

"To help others create better futures for themselves and those that they lead through teaching, speaking and writing." *Kris T.*

"My mission is to provide services/products in contract/ procurement to garner the best value for the Government for the American taxpayer." *Claudia W.*

"I help companies ensure they are providing competitive compensation, so they can adequately attract, retain, and motivate their employees." *Cassandra F.*

"My life's mission is to leave the world better than I found it. I want to make people's lives happy if I can impact them." *Shelley H.*

Each person has a slightly different perception of a mission. Some tie it directly to their field of expertise, a few see it as doing something, and others have a more generic view that involves showing up with people in a certain way.

The important piece to note is that there are different aspects to your mission. If you can answer the "what, how, and why" of your existence, then you are making good progress on understanding your mission.

Mission, Mindset, and Mouth Methodology

Composing your soul transcends beyond going to a peaceful place, it brings peace to every place.

When you know the ingredients that make up your mission, you develop a certain mindset.

Your mindset leads your mission to be expressed through your mouth and all of your messaging. It's what I call the Mission, Mindset, and Mouth Methodology. You live it, breathe it, and speak it.

Figuring out the mission isn't a linear process that starts at point A and ends at point B. I like to describe it as an ever-expanding circle. My logo for the School of Executive Presence is symbolic of the journey we are on.

There is a round center and hurricane pattern waves that move out from that circle. If you've ever been in a hurricane, you know it is so powerful to experience the extreme calm in the center. You also know those damaging winds can sling objects into the air, and you can be injured. The outskirts are for the people who run to avoid the whole experience.

You want to be in that circle. It's the eye of the storm. When you are in that circle, you can see everything going on around you, expand out your reach, and make waves that create impact. That circle moves along with the rest of the hurricane. If you run for the outskirts, then you are missing out on experiencing the fullness of your mission.

Thinking Beyond Your Job Title

You are more than your job title.

It's time now to start thinking of yourself beyond your current job title at work or home. You can probably spout off a bunch of titles that fit you depending on what situation you are in. For example, you may be all of the following:

Manager
Performer
Parent
Grandparent
Cook
Logistics Coordinator
Coach
Budget Analyst
Housekeeper
Dog Walker

The list is endless, but here is the truth: These titles don't necessarily define who you are at the core of your natural algorithm. When you are discovering and developing your mission, it's refreshing to know that you don't have to limit your life. You don't even have to work at the same company your entire life.

Fifty years ago, it was the prestigious and stable thing to do. In today's world, it is much more acceptable to explore different roles, and even move into niche markets through entrepreneurialism. As far as your current employment status is concerned, your job is only a tool for your mission. You don't have to go, but you don't have to stay.

What's important now is to bring your real title to the surface, the one defined by the elements of your natural algorithm.

How do you do this?

1. Do the work in this book.
2. Capture your reflections in your journal.
3. Pay close attention to pre-existing conditions, written code, and inner committee, and how they show up.
4. Go back and review, looking for themes and patterns.
5. Listen for what people notice about you, and what they come to you for.

I went through a similar process when I decided to open my consulting firm. I knew I needed to create my personal brand and simplify what my work was about. As a result, I found a few titles that I went as far as getting them trademarked:

Corporate Talent Expert®
Talent Remodeler®

Before I got to these refined titles, I went through a creative process to capture variations of who I am. I had some titles that were silly and fun, but then I got down to business. Other titles I came up with (and use from time to time) include:

- VIP Strategist (Visibility, Influence, and Presence)
- Perceptions Shifter
- Executive Presence Coach
- Confidence and Social Agility Guide

Creating your new titles will help activate your mission and give you a place to start describing who you are, what you do, and what value you bring.

Exercise: Create Your New Titles

This is a great exercise to capture in your journal over the next few days:

1. Review everything that you've reflected on as you have worked through the book.
2. Write down different words or ideas that come to you as you read.
3. Start stringing together the words, which can include adjectives, action words, and talent or skill words.
4. Come up with at least ten different titles.
5. Start to narrow them down as much as you can.
6. Revisit this every so often to nail down what title fits you best.
7. Once you create titles, create how you might introduce yourself using the following formula:
   - Introduce yourself with one of your titles.
   - Explain what you do, or what your title means.
   - Share what value you bring to the world.
   - Finish with why this is important.

This is fun and productive as you kick start your way into discovering your mission.

A Final Word About Your Mission

Gaining clarity on your mission is a big undertaking, so I don't want you to take this lightly. I've explained some basic directions to move toward. There are still things you just have to do to activate your mission, like breaking away from your normal routine.

Instead of going from home to work, and then back home, take a detour. Go somewhere where there are people. Go some place where you can have some quiet time. Play a quick game of putt-putt golf.

Go into a walk-in nail salon and get your feet scrubbed or nails painted. See who you meet. Or have dinner with a friend you haven't spoken to in a while. Request a 360-feedback assessment for yourself at work. Do something to search out your mission. Sitting at home wishing you knew what your mission is won't make it magically appear.

Remember, a mission isn't a place you go to, it's something you bring to every place. Yet, you can find clues by going places to explore. Start calling it forth, and it will faithfully show up.

CONCLUSION

"If I can overcome, anyone can."

-Angie Nuttle

"Okay, how do you end a book?"

I ask myself this question as if I have never done it before. I look to my natural algorithm for an answer, and I am reminded that I am a person who likes to keep going and going. For your sake, I won't rattle on, but I do want to leave you with something meaningful and inspirational. So, I have landed on this one last personal story for you from 1998 when I was a newly single mom experiencing freedom for the first time in a long time. It's a time when I started realizing that I had a mission and I needed to fight for it.

STORY: From Welfare to Wal-Mart to Wall Street

"Mama, I need $3.00 to watch a video at school, or they are going to make me sit in the cafeteria while everybody else watches the video."

It's my blonde haired little boy, Jared, who is embarrassed at the thought of being the only 3rd grader who can't pay to watch a video with his class. I am already annoyed that I rented that same movie a few months prior.

I am feeling embarrassed too because I don't even have 50 cents in my purse. The school has nickel and dimed me, and I haven't received any child support in months. We have a roof over our heads and some food in the cabinets, but that is about it. My daughter, Jazmin, is nearby and looking at me with her huge brown eyes. Everyone is silent, and I am trying to think. An idea hits me.

"Hop in the car; we're going to Wal-Mart."

The kids are giddy with questions.

"Why are we going to Wal-Mart? Are we going to get a toy? Can I get something?"

Quietly, I am praying that God will pull us through this one. I know He can, but lately, it's been tough to have much faith. As we pull up to the parking lot, I park and turn around to the kids.

"We are going to do something fun. We are getting out and walking around the parking lot to see who can find the most change."

Now, they are pumped as they hop out of the car. For Jazmin and Jared, everything is a competition, and this challenge is no different. I tell them to stay close by so they don't get run over by a car. And we begin the search.

Within a few short minutes, Jazmin is the first one to find a quarter. Right after that, Jared finds a dime. We pick up a few pennies here and there; then we consistently start picking up quarters, dimes, and nickels.

After an hour passes, we stop to count the change. It turns out that we have exactly $3.00.

"Woo-hoo!"

We are all hooting and hollering, joyously celebrating the achievement of our goal. We get in the car, go home, and have supper. Later, as I put all the change in Jared's envelope for his movie, a deep sense of sadness overwhelms me.

"Lord, why? Why does it have to be so hard?"

I automatically start to process my life's history, reliving some very ugly memories. The road has been rough. A tough childhood with trauma, being in foster care, running for my life, a drug addicted husband who drove me into bankruptcy and left me with a broken heart. Here I stand, thinking of everything. I could easily be a victim.

Somehow I know that all of the experiences are not in vain. They mean something. They might even be meant for someone else. Maybe I am supposed to share them.

"Lord, I never want to be in this position ever again."

At this moment, a wave of strength and resolve comes over me. I am determined to overcome this and help people like me. I don't know how I will get there, but I will do it.

I've made a decision to change my outcomes. More importantly, I have decided to learn more about what I am designed to do, and do it.

A few years later, I am working in Iraq as an HR defense contractor. I also go to work for a couple of Fortune 500 companies, but that isn't the success story. The success is that I chose to not wander in the wilderness of work aimlessly. All of my experiences have led me to where I am today, a businesswoman who is rocking it in the business world and living my mission. I am finally learning to align with my natural algorithm.

It's your turn.

You are now at a critical decision point. What are you going to choose to do? After all, you have been through, what will you move toward? You have choices in every situation. Will you choose to stay exactly as you are today? Will you decide to go to the opposite end of the spectrum by jumping off the cliff into a completely different direction?

Whatever you choose, it will change the course of your life forever. Decide bravely and wisely.

What about other people? I recommend that you stop focusing on other people and what they've done to you or how they've hurt you. They have a different algorithm. You are in a race with yourself. Focus on you so that you can be valuable for someone else.

My other last word of advice? Let me know if you need help getting out of prison. That's what I tell all my clients, and that is what I am here for. That applies to you too.

You can visit and connect with me at www.schoolofep.com or www.corporatetalentinstitute.com.

Just a heads up that I might be in Saint George Island at my future beach house overlooking the Gulf of Mexico. I will be painting a beautiful mural as I soak up the sun and write in my journal.

Then the Overly Productive Person in me will show up, take over, and concoct new ways to live a more elaborate mission. Don't worry; I will get back to you. My value of responsiveness won't hold me captive for long.

Oh, wait! I forgot one more thing: Don't quit. Just do something else.

ACKNOWLEDGEMENTS

Recognizing people is important. There are a special few who contributed to the writing of this book that I want to thank:

Jazmin Harper, my beautiful and smart oldest daughter, helped me in the early stages of writing. Her enthusiasm and genuine feedback inspired me to keep writing.

Aaron Nuttle, who always gives me the best material to work with when I need to give a practical illustration.

Kris Taylor, a good friend, mentor, and colleague who first introduced me to the concept of "Pillars"

My editor, Liz Thompson, who made the hard parts of writing easy through her gentle coaching.

My Lord and Savior, Jesus Christ, who has me on this Isaiah 61 Mission. He gives me purpose and joy.

CPSIA information can be obtained
at www.ICGtesting.com
Printed in the USA
LVOW09*1022110618
580301LV00015B/328/P